PATRIOTS POINT

IN REMEMBRANCE

Unless noted, all photographs are by the
Patriots Point Naval and Maritime Museum

LIBRARY OF CONGRESS
CATALOG NUMBER: 99-70715

ISBN: 1-57510-057-6

published for
Patriots Point Development Authority
by Pictorial Histories Publishing Co., Inc.
713 South Third Street West, Missoula, MT 59801

PATRIOTS POINT

IN REMEMBRANCE

by STEVE EWING

Patriots Point Artist in Residence since 1979, David Clark conveys power and emotion in his historically accurate depictions of significant historic naval and maritime events. Presented here are two of his paintings, one re-creating the 26 April 1952 collision between Wasp (CV-18) and Hobson (DMS-26), and the other (above) showing the last kamikaze hit on Enterprise (CV-6) 14 May 1945.

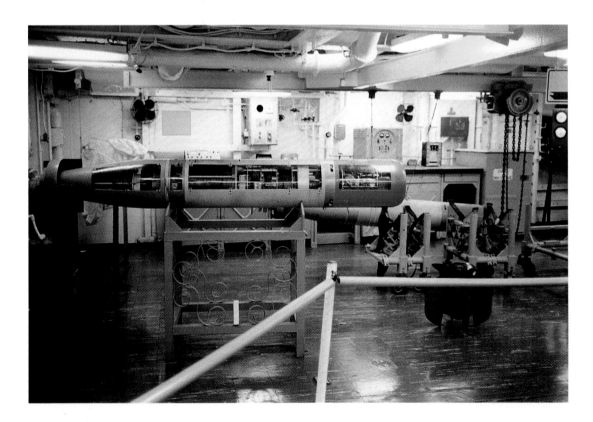

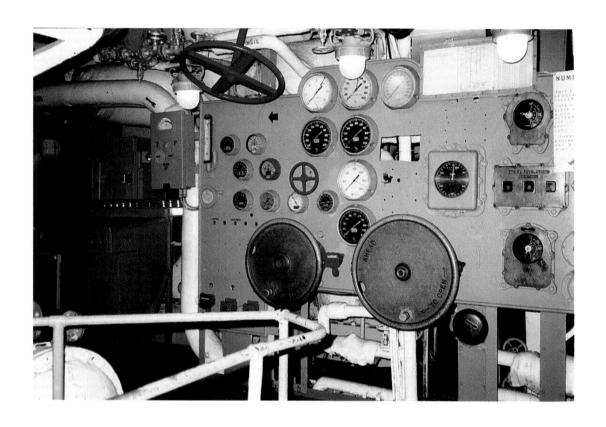

Contents

INTRODUCTION

O N 29 MARCH 1973, Governor John C. West approved legislation creating the Patriots Point Development Authority. Among the provisions of the legislation were powers to provide a place of education and recreation to foster pride and patriotism in the United States, and to establish and develop a National Naval Museum of ships, naval and maritime equipment, artifacts, books, art and other historical materials to tell the story of the importance of sea power. In 1975 the first ship for the museum was acquired and on 3 January 1976 the famous World War II aircraft carrier USS *Yorktown* (CV-10) was opened to the public at its pier in Mt. Pleasant. In 1981 the submarine USS *Clamagore* (SS-343), the decorated World War II destroyer USS *Laffey* (DD-724) and the nuclear powered merchant/passenger ship NS *Savannah* docked at Patriots Point for permanent exhibit. In May 1990 the U.S. Coast Guard Cutter *Ingham* joined the Patriots Point fleet to round out the composition of the Naval and Maritime Museum. NS *Savannah* was reluctantly returned to the Maritime Administration in 1994 in an effort to reduce Patriots Point's tremendous maintenance and restoration workload.

Among the first sights greeting visitors to Patriots Point is the relative size of the four ships, the large number of airplanes and exhibits and even the escalator between the hangar deck and flight deck of the aircraft carrier *Yorktown*. Among the first questions often asked are: "Was this *Yorktown* named for the carrier *Yorktown* sunk at Midway?" And "Why doesn't the *Yorktown's* escalator work?" And "What is the white ship beside the destroyer?"

Indeed, there is a considerable difference in the size of the 41,000 ton, 888 foot *Yorktown* and the 2,200 ton, 376 foot destroyer *Laffey* and the even smaller submarine, *Clamagore*. *Yortown* (CV-10) was named in honor of the gallant *Yorktown* (CV-5) lost at Midway. The *Yorktown's* escalator will work, but as the carrier is deemed a "building" because she is permanently moored in the mud, the 1950s era escalator does not meet contemporary OSHA standards. The white ship, *Ingham* is one of the most famous vessels ever to serve the Coast Guard. And, although many visitors recognize the *Laffey* as being a destroyer, few know her significant combat history.

First sights and natural questions aside, all that is immediately apparent to a visitor does not begin to convey the essence of the Naval and Maritime Museum's primary reason in being. For the most part, contemporary Americans cannot understand or appreciate the depth of feeling some other societies have for war as no recent war has been fought on American soil. With the meaning of duty, honor, sacrifice, deprivation and the horror of war not fully comprehensible, Patriots Point's mission is—in part—to educate visitors to the axiom that "freedom isn't free." To underscore this reality the museum, in a setting of historic ships and planes, presents remembrance of sailors, marines and airmen who met earlier challenges to America's freedom.

In sum, Patriots Point is a memorial museum. In the peaceful setting of Charleston Harbor, remembrance is offered not only to recognize the significant contributions of earlier patriots but also to pre-condition contemporary and future generations of Americans for the sacrifices they may be called upon to make in a continuing troubled world.

A print displaying a flight helmet mirroring burning Japanese carriers represents those lost in the Midway exhibit for whom photographs were unavailable. —JOE CASON

1
Remembrance of Those
Who Did Not Come Back

HIS NAME WAS JOHN UDELL LANE. Most likely, you never heard of him. No doubt a vast majority of naval historians would not recognize his name. But his name was particularly significant to his girlfriend and the immediate family to which he never returned.

On the morning of 4 June 1942 RM2c John Lane, looking backwards over his .30 caliber machine-gun, rode down the deck of the USS *Enterprise* (CV-6) in a TBD "Devastator" torpedo plane. Over the Japanese fleet during that day's momentous Battle of Midway, he and his pilot, Lt. (jg) John T. Eversole, crashed into the Pacific Ocean as a result of enemy action. Never again did his girlfriend, parents and other fam-

ily members see his face or share the warmth of his presence. There was no opportunity to see him in death, no opportunity to carry him to his grave and no opportunity to place a cemetery marker in his memory.

Viewing a body and cemetery markers not only provide honor to the deceased but also bring a sense of closure and a beginning of healing. In time, those left behind grasp and hold to a flood of happy memories. On special occasions or whenever an urge moves one to do so, a pilgrimage is made to the graves of loved ones. And there, sometimes resting against or touching the markers, one is emotionally reunited with those who have crossed the bridge from this life.

John Udell Lane and his family. —LANE FAMILY

While some of John Lane's family did not live to see the establishment of Patriots Point Naval and Maritime Museum in the mid-1970s, others have come aboard the *Yorktown*—flagship of the museum—to achieve what they were unable to do in 1942. John Lane's name is cast on a large bronze plaque honoring him and all others lost from the *Enterprise* during World War II. A large, unique exhibit on *Yorktown's* hangar deck recalls the Battle of Midway which changed the course of the war in the Pacific. And, on the second deck of *Yorktown* is a compartment honoring the wartime history of his carrier, the *Enterprise*.

Over 8,000 men who lost their lives in combat while serving on aircraft carriers in World War II, Korea, Vietnam and more recent conflicts, have their names engraved aboard *Yorktown*. All the carriers that earned battle stars or steamed in harm's way are also memorialized. Over 300,000 come each year to visit the ships of Patriots Point, and among those many are a few who come to see a special name on a special plaque. For these

few, Patriots Point is more than an interesting museum full of ships, aircraft and artifacts: it is a place of closure, of healing and memories.

We believe RM2c John Udell Lane would be pleased.

The National Memorial to Carrier Aviation

WHILE THE NATIONAL MEMORIAL to Carrier Aviation, often referred to as the "Arlington of Carrier Aviation," was created to remember John Udell Lane and over 8,000 other naval and marine aviators and sailors, RM2c Lane was not the initial inspiration. That distinction belongs to Lt. E. T. "Smokey" Stover, USNR. The 24 year old pilot, a gentle person who loved classical music and literature, had distinguished himself in aerial combat early in the war shooting down four Japanese planes. Only a week after recording the 7,000th landing on *Yorktown* in February 1944,

The "Arlington of Carrier Aviation" consoles and plaques present the names of over 8,000 navy and marine aviators lost in combat operations while serving aboard U.S. Navy carriers.

Exterior of the "Smokey Stover Memorial Theatre" on Yorktown's *hangar deck.*

"Smokey" flew his F6F Hellcat fighter off the deck of CV-10 to attack Truk, the Japanese "Pearl Harbor." Most of his fellow pilots in VF-5 (Fighting Squadron Five) returned to the carrier, but "Smokey" did not. Best evidence is that he was shot down, captured, interrogated and then executed. Years later the pain of his loss motivated the leadership of the Yorktown Association (veterans of the carrier) to create a proper memorial to assure remembrance of both the young man and his deeds.

At the fifth reunion of the Yorktown Association in New York City 15 April 1952, the veterans presented a plaque to "Smokey's" parents. That small but meaningful ceremony helped ease some of the feeling of his loss, but it was not enough. On 26 January 1957 a bronze plaque honoring "Smokey" was placed aboard the still active carrier. That too helped, but still it was not enough. After the ship was decommissioned and transferred to the State of South Carolina in 1975 to become a museum, one of the first efforts of the *Yorktown* veter-

ans was to transform the carrier's elevator well in Hangar Bay One into a theater wherein the 1944 Academy Award winning movie, "The Fighting Lady" could be shown. While all World War II aircraft carriers were "fighting ladies," *Yorktown* took the sobriquet as her own as most of the movie was filmed on her decks. The new theater aboard *Yorktown* was named "Stover Theater," but even this was not enough. Finally, the idea surfaced to create a national memorial to carrier aviation, an "Arlington" wherein all the names of those who manned U.S. Navy carriers and their air groups and died in combat or in combat related duties would have a place of sacred remembrance. There were many "Smokey Stovers" who did not return, and until establishment of the *Yorktown* "Arlington," their final resting places were noted only by a latitude and longitude entry in the pages of their respective ship's log filed in the National Archives. A proper memorial would not erase the pain of loss, but it would make the loss bearable by preserving the meaning of the sacrifice and sharing the blessings of peace and freedom that have resulted.

Despite the apparent difficulties in finding all the names of men lost while serving on carriers, the *Yorktown* veterans vowed to accept the challenge and carry it through to fruition. The challenge was as difficult as expected. Being nearly impossible to find all the names in the surviving documents from the carriers, research was also necessary from other sources. A continuing problem was tracking names of men who were wounded aboard a carrier but who died on another ship. While researching names was sufficient difficulty within itself, money had to be raised to fund the plaques, which cost $1,000 to $15,000. As nearly 100 carriers had been commissioned in the U.S. Navy since the seven in commission when World War II began, it was apparent that approximately 100 plaques would be required to complete the permanent memorial. Both the records research and the fund raising proved to be laborious, but it was a labor of deep emotional commitment. When names were elusive and donors reticent, the *Yorktown* veterans pressed on, driven by the memory of "Smokey" and the knowledge that thousands like him lost on distant islands or buried at sea had no gravestone or tangible marker to record their sacrifice.

On 21 October 1979 the first bronze plaques,

Close-up view of the bronze "Arlington" plaque honoring the officers and men lost while serving on the first aircraft carrier Yorktown (CV-5).

some large, some small, were dedicated. Presently, 104 plaques have been dedicated. Still, new names are being found and small addendum plaques are being attached to the large, light blue circular consoles upon which they are mounted. Naval Aviation's equivalent of the Vietnam Wall in Washington, DC, the "Arlington" aboard *Yorktown* serves the same healing purpose. Children point to the plaques asking explanation from their parents, veterans point to certain names with simultaneous feelings of pride, sadness and joy, and family members touch the raised lettering, usually in silence as words are not equal to the emotions of the moment.

Is the National Memorial to Carrier Aviation complete? Will there be a need to add more names to the 8,080 already placed? It is just as well that the answer is currently not known. It is doubtful that any of those lost ever expected to die when they first reported aboard their respective aircraft carrier. Certainly no one ever expected to have the "Arlington" aboard *Yorktown* stand in place of a cemetery marker.

When visiting the National Memorial to Carrier Aviation in Hangar Bay One aboard *Yorktown*, guests cannot help noticing that several carriers suffered considerably more than others. *Franklin* (CV-13), *Bunker Hill* (CV-17) and *Liscome Bay* (CVE-56) lost so many that multiple large plaques were required to list all

RADM James "Pop" Condit, USN, Ret., leads a procession of former CV-10 crewmembers and guests to the carrier's port side to place wreath's over the side in honor of departed veterans. —YORKTOWN ASSOCIATION

their names. Guests also notice that carrier plaques with only a few names speak to the inherent danger of carrier operations. While most men were lost as a result of enemy action, others were lost as returning aircraft smashed into parked planes or landed in catwalks. Some moved into propeller blades, some received fatal injuries while fueling or arming aircraft and some were lost overboard. To those left behind, the cause of death was relatively insignificant. Premature death leaves an indelible void that disappears only when those left behind cross the bridge from this life to the next. But until that day the National Memorial to Carrier Aviation assures remembrance.

Battle of Midway Carrier Torpedo Squadrons Memorial

HOW BEST TO HONOR the memory of a person or event? A speech? Exhibit? Book? Movie? Whether speech, exhibit, book or movie, the essence of the 4 June 1942 Battle of Midway will continue to capture the imagination of all interested in naval history. The elements of any good story—suspense, underdogs, courage, luck, chance, secrecy and secrecy revealed, failure and success—were expressed in that momentous battle. During those three days of battle were thousands of individual trials, tribulations and victories.

Present for the October 1988 dedication of the Midway exhibit were four of six then living Midway torpedo squadron survivors. From left: George Gay (VT-8); Capt. Albert Earnest, USN, Ret., (VT-8 Detached); Commander W.G. Esders (VT-3); and RADM R E. Laub (VT-6). Into 1998 only Capt. Earnest survives. Patriots Point's Dr. Steve Ewing is at the podium.

Torpedo Squadron Three (VT-3) immediately before the Battle of Midway.
Half those pictured here were killed in action days later.   —USN

As intriguing as the individual stories were, the most compelling episode continues to be the story of the U.S. Navy carrier torpedo squadron (VT) attacks on 4 June. Although more than 50 years have passed, that heroic aerial charge has become a part of American military folklore equivalent to the British 19th century "Charge of the Light Brigade."

The pilots and radioman-gunners who remain forever young from that day are remembered for demonstrating the epitome of duty, courage and sacrifice. The pilots of the Douglas TBD Devastators were confronted by Japanese Zero fighters nearly three times faster. Even without the variance in respective aircraft speed, the TBD pilots would still have had to slow to "sitting-duck" speed to drop their slow, unreliable Mark XIII torpedoes. Additionally, every

Japanese ship in sight was shooting at them, and the TBDs few escorting Wildcat fighters were either unable to engage or were intercepted by Zeros. Nonetheless, they pressed their attack.

All 15 planes of VT-8 from *Hornet* (CV-8) were shot down; 10 of the 12 of VT-3 flying from *Yorktown* (CV-5) were lost; and 10 of 14 VT-6 TBDs failed to return to *Enterprise* (CV-6). Flying from Midway were six new TBF Avengers (VT-8 detached): only one returned.

Few examples in American military history offer a more dramatic example of sacrifice. The crews of the torpedo planes who died that day forfeited over 16,000 future sunsets, more than 50,000 meals, and the opportunity to share countless expressions of affection. This reality was not lost on those who quickly recognized the impossible mission before them on 4 June

The "Battle of Midway Carrier Torpedo Squadrons Memorial" aboard Yorktown.

1942, but their sacrifice often appears lost on subsequent generations of Americans who have enjoyed the fruits of victory and peace.

On 11 October 1987, four survivors of the torpedo squadrons that fought at Midway came to Patriots Point for the dedication of a permanent memorial exhibit honoring them and their shipmates who did not return. By 1987 only five members of the Midway torpedo squadrons were still living. By coincidence, there was one from each of the three carrier squadrons and one from the detached VT-8 squadron that flew from Midway.

Captain Albert "Bert" Earnest, the only TBF pilot to survive the battle, represented VT-8 (detached): George Gay, the sole survivor of VT-8 from *Hornet*, was present as was Commander W.G. "Bill" Esders of VT-3 from *Yorktown* and Rear Admiral Robert Laub of VT-6 from *Enterprise*.

During the 11 October ceremony George Gay and "Bert" Earnest declined to speak at length, stating that no words could be equal to

the sacrifice made by the other members of their squadron on 4 June 1942. RADM Laub, one of five VT-6 pilots to survive the battle and one of four to return to the "Big E," paid tribute to his fallen squadron-mates but abridged his speech as the remembrance opened old emotional scars. Commander Esders, however, spoke at length. One of only two pilots from his squadron to survive the battle, Esders paid homage to the pilots and gunners of his and other squadrons in a moving speech. He recounted how his rear seat gunner died in his arms after he crashed landed alongside the fatally wounded *Yorktown*, briefly noted how he had to assume command when his squadron leader (Lt. Commander "Lem" Massey) was shot down, and he offered special praise to the memory of then Lt. Commander John S. Thach (later Admiral) of *Yorktown's* VF-3 for his advice on how to defend against enemy fighters while flying the TBD. "He told us," said Esders, "to fly low against the water, fly as slow as possible, let them shoot at you, and then turn toward the Zero just before the projectiles hit." Using this tactic several times, one Zero, apparently out of ammunition, flew up beside Esders and waved. Esders could only interpret the wave as meaning "you live because you earned it."

The many words of Esders, the emotions of Laub and the few words of Earnest and Gay were all equally eloquent. For the purpose of preserving history, the greatest eloquence was simply their presence on 11 October 1987. At the time of this writing in late 1996, only Captain Earnest has not left this world to rejoin his squadron-mates.

The exhibit Earnest, Gay, Esders and Laub helped dedicate aboard *Yorktown* is focused on the torpedo squadron officers and men who died at Midway. A framed picture and engraved plate serve as an "Arlington" for the men lost at sea, and serves to remind visitors how young and how full of life they were. A search of official naval records, and requests to family, friends and reunion groups was necessary to gather individual photographs. A few could not be located. In place of an unavailable photograph is a print of an original rendering by the late Joe Cason depicting a flight helmet floating on the water. In the lens of the helmet, one can see a mirror effect of Japanese carriers aflame on the horizon.

Resting in one of the display cases alongside the original Cason rendering is one of the last letters written to his wife by VT-8 commanding officer, Lt. Commander John Waldron. The letter closes with Waldron's assurance that "It will all come out well, I am sure." Fully aware of the challenge before him, Waldron told his men before the battle "If there is only one plane left to make a final run-in, I want that man to go in and get a hit." He then added, "May God be with us all."

Several other artifacts and displays in this exhibit have drawn considerable attention from

This small section of fuselage on display in the Midway exhibit is the only known extant piece of a TBD Devastator that flew into the battle.

visitors. When the late Commander Stephen B. Smith of VT-6 landed back aboard *Enterprise* on 4 June 1942, his plane was so badly damaged it was considered worthy only of being pushed over the side. While others were counting the dozens of bullet holes in the TBD, Smith busied himself by cutting off a small painting from the fuselage. The 18x24 inch painting of a black cat with yellow letters spelling "SCAT" rests in a display case, the only known surviving part of a TBD that flew at Midway.

Other items of special interest are two Navy Crosses (Esders and Laub), a large scratch-built model of a TBD crafted by John Ficklen, and large dioramas of the U.S. Navy and Japanese striking forces at Midway crafted by James Grigerick and Tom Arusiewicz. Nearly all children are immediately drawn to the models. Adults walk directly to the pictures of Waldron, Massey, Lindsey, Ely, Riley, Hart, Osmus . . .

Missing in Action-Prisoner of War Display

MUCH SMALLER IN SIZE than either the "Arlington" or "Midway" memorials is a display calling attention to veterans of recent wars who are still listed as missing or are prisoners of war. Some of these men may eventually return, but the probability is that few if any ever will. Located in the Coppi Aviation Ordnance Memorial Armory immediately inside *Yorktown's* island beside the flight deck, only two items are on display, but they are enough to convey a strong message.

The familiar black and white MIA-POW flag tells as much of a story and elicits as much emotion as any national flag. It reminds one and all that some American servicemen are not accounted for from World War II, Korea and especially, Vietnam.

Displayed beneath the MIA-POW flag is a diorama of the "Vietnam Alcatraz." This prison was the home more than 26 months for 11 POWs who led the resistance movement of American POWs held in North Vietnam. They were kept in solitary confinement and leg irons, and were completely isolated from the POW community. Each cell had three solid walls, a solid door and concrete floor. The 10×4½ foot area was divided into a raised 6×4½ foot area for sleeping and a 4×4½ foot area for normal living and exercise space. Two of the 11 became nationally famous after release in 1973; Senator Jeremiah D. Denton (R. Alabama), and Medal of Honor recipient and vice presidential candidate, Vice Admiral James B. Stockdale.

2

Remembrance of Those Who Excelled

Congressional Medal of Honor Museum

OVER 120 RECIPIENTS and several hundred spectators were present 28 October 1993 for the formal dedication of The National Congressional Medal of Honor Museum aboard the aircraft carrier *Yorktown*. Ceremonies marked the first time many of the recipients of the nation's highest honor had visited Patriots Point and toured the new exhibit. The event was part of a week-long national convention of the Congressional Medal of Honor Society, held for the first time in Mt. Pleasant and Charleston, South Carolina.

The new Medal of Honor Museum is located on the hangar deck of the *Yorktown* near the main entrance of the ship, and features displays representing the eight eras for which the medal has been awarded. Exhibits also include several Medals of Honor, artifacts and memorabilia related to recipients, original paintings by Patriots Point Artist in Residence, David A. Clark, original black and white renderings by the late Joe Cason, and citations describing the actions for which the coveted meals were awarded. In addition to numerous paper items related to recipients, artifacts of interest include an ashtray from the sunken submarine *Squalus* (SS-192) from which 33 of 59 crewmembers were rescued in 1939 thanks to the heroic actions of several Medal of Honor recipients, uniforms, weapons, a bible and other personal items carried in combat by recipients.

Some of the recipients names are familiar to many who visit the exhibit. Charles Lindbergh, first man to fly alone across the Atlantic; Audie Murphy, whose combat heroism translated into a movie career; "Butch" O'Hare, for whom the Chicago International Airport is named, and Sgt. Alvin C. York of World War I fame, are but a few. Capt. Tom Custer's name is often recognized as he was a brother to "General" George Custer. Both died at Little Big Horn in 1876. But, most of the recipients are unknown even to serious students of American history, and some like Sgt. Jim, an Indian scout, are remembered in the Medal of Honor Society's records only by name and the brief wording of their citation. While some of the citations are long enough to describe the actions and valor of a recipient, many state only "bravery in action." Still, stories of great human interest are apparent to visitors who read the few selected citations on display. Especially unique is that of Sgt. Thomas Higgins. During the 1863 Battle of Vicksburg, Higgins carried the American flag across a battlefield while musket and cannon fire killed scores around him. As his fellow soldiers fell, Higgins continued on, unarmed except for the flag. As he neared the Confederate positions, the rebels called out to one another not to shoot the brave flag-bearer. Perhaps the only soldier ever captured amid cheers from his enemy, Higgins received the Medal of Honor after a delegation of Southern veterans traveled to post-war Washington to recommend him for the decoration..

The Medal of Honor Society maintains their national office in a suite immediately beside the exhibit, and assists with solicitation of memora-

Consoles within the Congressional Medal of Honor Society Museum aboard Yorktown *represent the eight eras from which the medal has been awarded.*

bilia for the exhibit. Design for the interior of the exhibit and the financing for its construction was provided by Patriots Point. The exhibits serve to educate visitors of the contributions and sacrifices made in defense of the United States and consequent "above and beyond" individual awards. The eight display consoles along the interior curved wall represent the Civil War, Indian Campaigns, Wars of American Expansion, Peacetime, World War I, World War II, Korea and Vietnam. Each console displays photographs and engraved citations for selected recipients.

At the top of each console, the number of recipients for each war or era is noted. Of the total 3,399 recipients (as of October 1993: two awards have since been made for Somalia and seven black soldiers who served in World War II were added 13 January 1997, plus others are under review), the Civil War ranks highest with 1,520. Only 123 were awarded during World War I. The total number of medals awarded to date is 3,418 as 19 recipients received the medal twice. Names of the recipients are listed by war or era both inside the exhibit and on exterior panels. Land-side, the Medal of Honor Society has assisted youth groups with tree plantings in honor of recipients.

Yorktown Carrier Aviation Hall of Fame

THE YORKTOWN Carrier Aviation Hall of Fame was established in 1981 to honor carrier combat heroes, outstanding carrier-force leaders, and captain's of industry who designed carrier-based aircraft plus those who produced aircraft carriers. Plaque inscriptions were authored by the Yorktown Association, who originated and has since sponsored the Hall of Fame. On many of the plaques inscriptions were abbreviated, and "understood" words omitted to conserve space. Inscriptions produced herein have been selectively changed to facilitate understanding of naval terminology and to fill-in "understood" words. And, it is known that some have died (*) since their induction, but dates of death are included only if the exact year is known.

FRANK AKERS
Rear Admiral, U.S. Navy
1901–*

Commanded Navy fighter training, 1928–31. The pioneer in aviation electronics, communications, and instrument flying. Made first "blind" landing on a carrier, the USS *Langley* CV-1, in July 1935. Directed design of all VHF radio, night fighter radar and other vital electronic equipment in U.S. carrier forces, 1942–45. Captain of the *Saratoga* CV-3, 1945–46. Elected to Carrier Hall of Fame 1981.

RICHARD H. BEST
Lieutenant Commander, U.S. Navy
1910–

1936 VF-2 "Chiefs" Squadron in *Lexington* CV-2. 1940 ordered to *Enterprise* CV-6: flight officer VB-6. Feb. 1ˢᵗ, 1942 as XO Bombing Six led attack on Marshalls, the first carrier raid of WWII. Awarded DFC. CO of VB-6 on 4 June 1942. Was one of the top performers at Battle of Midway as the first dive bomber pilot to hit one of the four Japanese carriers, the *Agaki*, and the only pilot to score a second hit, on the *Hiryu*, thus helping sink two of the carriers that had led the 7 December attack on Pearl Harbor. Inhalation of caustic soda from a defective oxygen canister during first Midway strike resulted in TB and medical retirement in 1944. Elected to Carrier Hall of Fame in 1993.

WILLIAM EDWARD BLEWETT, JR.
Aircraft Carrier Shipbuilder
1895–1965

Dynamic official of the Newport News Shipbuilding and Dry Dock Company. As draughtsman, Supt. of Shipbuilding, President and Chairman of the Board, he participated in the construction of 19 carriers during the period 1934–1965, including CV-5 and CV-10 Yorktowns, the "Big E" CV-6, and *Enterprise* CVN-65, the world's first nuclear-powered carrier. Elected to Carrier Hall of Fame in 1981.

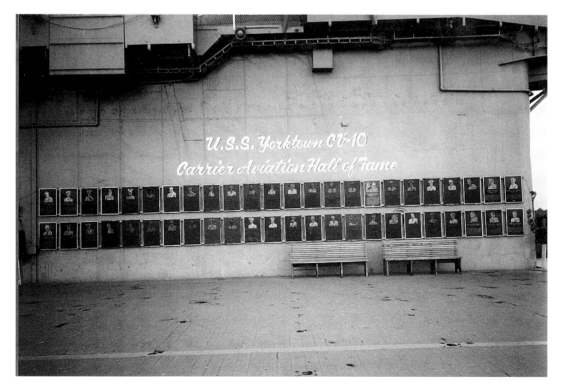

From 1981 through 1997, the Yorktown Carrier Aviation Hall of Fame was located on the port side of the carrier's island.

Hall of Fame Plaques for Fleet Admiral's Ernest J. King and William F. Halsey, and the Navy's top ace, Capt. David McCampbell.

WILLIAM OSCAR BRICE
Lieutenant General, U.S. Marine Corps
1898–1972

Father of Marine Corps carrier aviation. November 2, 1931, then Lt. Brice, CO of Marine Corps Scouting Squadron 15-M, took it aboard *Lexington* CV-2 and remained aboard until January 1933 operating brilliantly as an integral part of the Navy's air group. December 1942–January 1944, Brice, stationed on Guadalcanal, commanded all Marine and Navy combat aircraft in the Solomons including Tom Blackburn's famous Navy VF-17 skull & crossbones squadron. Brice served as director of all Marine Corps aviation 1953–55. Elected to Carrier Hall of Fame in 1989.

GODFREY deC. CHEVALIER
Lieutenant Commander, U.S. Navy
1889–1922

Assisted 1920–21 in converting the ex-collier, USS *Jupiter* into the Navy's first aircraft carrier which on 20 March 1922 at the Norfolk Navy Yard was commissioned USS *Langley* CV-1. While serving on board as the first officer in charge of the Langley's aviation detachment he was credited with developing the first landing deck gear. On 26 October 1922, off Cape Henry, he made the first landing on a ship underway, *Langley* CV-1. Elected to Carrier Hall of Fame in 1987.

J.J. "JOCKO" CLARK
Admiral, U.S. Navy
1893–1971

CO VF-2 in *Lexington* CV-2, 1931–33. XO *Yorktown* CV-5 May 1941–February 1942. CO *Suwannee* CVE-27 for invasion of North Africa. Commissioned *Yorktown* CV-10, 15 April 1943. A record 99 days later, CV-10 arrived at Pearl Harbor to start the new Pacific offensive with strikes on Marcus, Wake, Gilbert's and Marshalls. Mitscher's TF-58's premier group commander April 1944–June 1945. Battle of Philippine Sea, Jimas, Luzon, Tokyo, Kyushu, Kure, *Yamato*, Iwo Jima, Okinawa. Commanded TF-77 and 7th Fleet during Korean War, 1951–53. Elected to Carrier Hall of Fame in 1987.

JOHN G. CROMMELIN, JR.
Rear Admiral, U.S. Navy
1902–1996

Ranked in top five of carrier aviation's fighter and bomber pilots, 1929–39, VF-3 and VB-5 in *Lexington* CV-2; VF-3 and VB-4 in *Ranger* CV-4; CO VB-3 in *Saratoga* CV-3. Air Officer and XO of "The Big E" CV-6, June 1942–September 1943 and universally regarded as "Mr. Enterprise." Chief of Staff CarDiv's 24 and 12, September 1943–August 1944. Commanded *Saipan* CVL-48 July 1946–September 1947. In 1949 he sacrificed his 4.0 career by precipitating the "Air Admirals' Revolt" that saved carrier aviation. Elected to Carrier Hall of Fame in 1987.

ROBERT ELLINGTON DIXON
Read Admiral, U.S. Navy
1906–1981

Awarded two Navy Crosses as CO of VS-2 aboard *Lexington* CV-2, 7 December 1941–8 May 1942. After he and his squadron sank a Japanese carrier during the Battle of the Coral Sea, he sent the famous radio transmission: "Scratch one flattop." Operations Officer CarDiv One, October 1942–April 1944. Commanded *Palau* CVE-122, 1948–49 and *Valley Forge* CV-45 during the Korean War, 1952–53. Chief of Bureau of Aeronautics, January 1957–November 1959. Elected to Carrier Hall of Fame in 1984.

DONALD WILLS DOUGLAS
Carrier Airplane Builder
1892–1981

Founder of Douglas Aircraft Company in 1921, he produced many successful bombing and torpedo planes for U.S. aircraft carriers: the SBD Dauntless, which sank four Japanese carriers at the Battle of Midway: the AD Skyraider, workhorse of the Korean and Vietnam wars: and the

Retired Rear Admiral John G. Crommelin addresses the audience present for his induction into the Carrier Aviation Hall of Fame, October 1987.

A3D Skywarrior which in the 1950s gave the carriers a true nuclear weapons capability. Elected to Carrier Hall of Fame in 1981.

ARTHUR LATIMER DOWNING
Captain, U.S. Navy
1915–

Premier WWII carrier aviation dive bomber pilot. VS-5 in *Yorktown* CV-5, VS-5 in *Enterprise* CV-6, CO VB-14 in *Wasp* CV-18. Awarded 3 Navy Crosses, Silver Star, Bronze Star and 14 Air Medals for action at Lae and Salamaua, Tulagi, Coral Sea, Eastern Solomons, Santa Cruz, Marianas, Battle of the Philippine Sea, Jimas, Palau, Formosa, Luzon and Leyte Gulf. Scored first hit on *Yamato*. CAG-2 in *Boxer* CV-21 during Korean War, August 1951–October 1952. Elected to Carrier Hall of Fame in 1987.

DONALD BRADLEY DUNCAN
Admiral, U.S. Navy
1896–1975

In 1941 he pioneered development of the escort carrier and the composite squadron as CO of first ship converted to an escort carrier, USS *Long Island* CVE-1. He was the Navy's coordinator of Doolittle's B-25 raid on Tokyo from *Hornet* CV-8 on 18 April 1942. Commissioned December 1942 and through October 1943 was CO of *Essex* CV-9, first of 24 Essex class fast carriers. Commander Carrier Division's 4 and 5, July 1945–January 1946. Vice Chief of Naval Operations, 1951–1956. Elected to Carrier Hall of Fame in 1985.

ALBERT KYLE EARNEST
Captain, U.S. Navy
1917–

Premier WWII torpedo pilot with six torpedo combat missions. Received three Navy Crosses, two for one mission, an unprecedented award in the history of naval aviation. Attached to Hornet's VT-8 detachment flying the new TBF Avenger, he made the first attack on four Japanese carriers. Zero's shot down his fellow five pilots, riddled his plane and killed his gunner, but somehow he crash-landed back on Midway. In the Battle of the Eastern Solomons his torpedo hit helped sink the carrier *Ryujo*. From Guadalcanal he made four torpedo attacks on Japanese shipping. Elected to Carrier Hall of Fame in 1989.

Admiral Marc Mitscher (in uniform) and Secretary of the Navy James Forrestal were inducted into the Hall of Fame in 1982 and 1985 respectively. USN

JAMES H. "JIMMY" FLATLEY, JR.
Vice Admiral, U.S. Navy
1906–1958

One of carrier aviation's top fighter pilot tacticians, 1931–1942. XO of VF-42 on *Yorktown* CV-5 during Battle of the Coral Sea. Led VF-10 "Grim Reapers" on the "Big E" at Santa Cruz and November 1942–February 1943 from Guadalcanal. CAG-5 on *Yorktown* CV-10, he flew the first F6F Hellcat aboard. VADM Mitscher's fast carrier Task Force 58 Operations Officer, July 1944 to June 1945. 1952–56 he commanded *Block Island* CVE-106 and *Lake Champlain* CV-39 which won battle "E" pennants. Elected to Carrier Hall of Fame in 1982.

JAMES VINCENT FORRESTAL
Statesman
1892–1949

Naval Aviator # 154. Served as a Lieutenant during WWI. Under Secretary of the Navy 1940–1944. Entrusted by President Roosevelt to built two-ocean Navy including 19 CVs, 9 CVLs 75 CVEs and 35,000 carrier aircraft. Secretary of the Navy, May 1944–July 1947. As architect of Department of Defense and the National Security Council, he led the fight to keep carrier aviation under the control of the Navy. First Secretary of Defense, September 1947–March 1949. Elected to Carrier Hall of Fame in 1985.

BRUNO P. GAIDO
AMM1C, U.S. Navy
1916–1942

On 1 February 1942 during the first carrier raid of WWII, on Marshall-Gilberts, AMM2C Gaido, a radio-gunner in VS-6 aboard *Enterprise* CV-6, ran to his plane parked aft on the flight deck, and using the SBD's rear gun, exploded an enemy plane so close its wing cut off the SBD's tail. For his heroics, he received a commendation and promotion to AMM1C. Awarded the

Distinguished Flying Cross for the Battle of Midway 4 June 1942. After diving on one of the four Japanese carriers sunk that day, his SBD was forced to ditch. He and his pilot were picked up by an enemy destroyer, interrogated, weighted down and thrown over the side. His courage in combat and when facing death was exemplary. Elected to Carrier Hall of Fame in 1995.

LEROY RANDLE GRUMMAN
Carrier Airplane Builder
1895–*

Founded Grumman Aircraft Corporation in 1929. Produced the core of the Navy's carrier fighter planes over the next 50 years, notably, the F4F Wildcat and F6F Hellcat of World War II, F9F Panther of the Korean War, and the F-14 Tomcat of the 1970s. Grumman also built the TBF Avenger torpedo bomber, the A-6 Intruder attack plane, and S2F anti-submarine Tracker. Elected to Carrier Hall of Fame in 1981.

WILLIAM F. HALSEY, JR.
Fleet Admiral, U.S. Navy
1882–1959

Aggressive and inspirational carrier admiral who led the first U.S. Navy carrier raids in early 1942 against the Japanese Marshall and Gilbert Islands aboard his flagship, *Enterprise* CV-6. Commanded the carrier task force for the Doolittle raid against Tokyo, 18 April 1942. Commanded the Third Fleet August 1944–January 1945, and May–August 1945. Led the victorious U.S. Fleet into Tokyo Bay for surrender ceremonies, 2 September 1945. Elected to Carrier Hall of Fame in 1989.

CECIL ELWOOD HARRIS
Captain, U.S. Naval Reserve
1916–1981

The Navy's amazing World War II 24-kill mystery ace. A farm boy and hunter from Crespard,

South Dakota (pop. 500), Harris joined the Naval Reserve a year before Pearl Harbor. Flying from *Suwannee* CVE-27, he participated in the invasion of North Africa. Shot down his first two planes during the defense of Guadalcanal. Attached to VF-18 in *Intrepid* CV-11, in two months, September–November 1944 he shot down 22 more planes (17 Zeros in fierce dog fights). Awarded nine combat decorations: Navy Cross, two Silver Stars, three DFC's and three Air Medals. If CV-11 had not been hit 25 November 1944, Harris would have undoubtedly ended up as the Navy's and Marine Corps' leading ace. Elected as First Reserve into Carrier Hall of Fame in 1989.

VERNE W. "PAPPY" HARSHMAN
Lt. Commander, U.S. Navy
1902–*

During the 1930s carrier aviation's foremost "A.P." (Enlisted Naval Aviation Pilot) flying fighter and torpedo planes from *Langley* CV-1, *Lexington* CV-2, and *Saratoga* CV-3. His five days in a life raft pioneered development of survival at sea equipment which since 1931 has helped save hundreds of aviator's lives. WWII's premier flight deck and Assistant Air Officer while aboard *Yorktown* CV-10, 1943–1945. Elected to Carrier Hall of Fame 1983.

ARTHUR RAY HAWKINS
Captain, U.S. Navy
1922–

Awarded Navy Cross, three DFCs and three Air Medals attached to VF-31, May 1943–September 1945 aboard *Cabot* CVL-28 and *Belleau Wood* CVL-24. Participated in all naval engagements from the Marshall Islands operations to the fall of Japan. Tenth ranking WWII Navy ace with 14 planes. During Korean War he was awarded fourth Air Medal while serving as XO of VF-191 aboard *Princeton* CV-37. Commanded the Blue Angels August 1951–April 1954. Elected to Carrier Hall of Fame in 1984.

EDWARD H. HEINEMANN
Carrier Aircraft Designer
1908–1991

As Chief Engineer for Douglas Aircraft Company, Heinemann was the premier designer of carrier based aircraft, 1937–60. He designed the SBD Dauntless dive bomber, that "turned the tide at Midway" by sinking four Japanese carriers; the AD Skyraider attack bomber which was the "workhorse" of the Korean and Vietnam wars; F4D Skyray interceptor, winner of the 1953 Collier trophy; A3D Skywarrior, first carrier nuclear bomber: and A4D Skyhawk, carrier light jet attack bomber, 1954–79. Elected to Carrier Hall of Fame in 1987.

ARNOLD JAY ISBELL
Captain, U.S. Navy
1899–1945

Attached to VT-1B 1929–1931 on *Lexington* CV-2. Served on *Ranger* CV-4 and *Saratoga* CV-3 1933–36. Premier escort carrier commander, Atlantic Theatre, April 1943–March 1944. As Commander Task Unit 21.14 and *Card* CVE-11, his forces sank 10 German U-boats, 20% of total 52 credited to CVE hunter-killer task units. Ordered to command *Yorktown* CV-10. Six days before reporting, he was killed on *Franklin* CV-13, 19 March 1945. Elected to Carrier Hall of Fame in 1985.

HENRY JOHN KAISER
Aircraft Carrier Shipbuilder
1882–1967

Founder and Chairman of Kaiser Industries who during World War II built 50 of the Navy's escort carriers of the Casablanca CVE-55 class. These jeep carriers were the keystone of the hunter-killer groups that defeated the Nazi U-boats in the Atlantic; and providing close air support were essential in the Pacific during the invasions of Tarawa, Saipan, Guam, the Philippines, Iwo Jima and Okinawa. Elected to Carrier Hall of Fame 1983.

ERNEST JOSEPH KING
Fleet Admiral, U.S. Navy
1878–1956

Captain of the *Lexington* CV-2 (1930–32). Chief of the Bureau of Aeronautics (1933–36). Commander of the Fleet's carriers (1938–39). He helped prepare carrier aviation for war. As Commander-In-Chief United States Fleet and Chief of Naval Operations during World War II Admiral King was the principal strategist in the victory over Japan. Elected to Carrier Hall of Fame in 1981.

MAXWELL F. LESLIE
Rear Admiral, U.S. Navy
1902–1985

Member of VF-5 in *Lexington* CV-2 and *Ranger* CV-4, 1935–38. Ordered in May 1940 to *Saratoga* CV-3 as XO of VB-3 until the *Saratoga* was torpedoed on 11 January 1942. VB-3 with Leslie promoted to CO was then transferred to *Enterprise* CV-6 which escorted *Hornet* CV-8 on Doolittle Raid on Tokyo 18 April 1942. Operating from *Yorktown* CV-5 on 4 June 1942, Leslie was one of the Battle of Midway's major heroes and Navy Cross winners, leading his VB-3 Squadron of 17 SBDs in a dive bombing attack on the enemy's four carriers scoring three hits on *Soryu*, setting her afire and sinking her. In August 1942 as CO of Air Group 6 in *Enterprise*, Leslie led his air group during the invasion of Guadalcanal and the Battle of the Eastern Solomons. Elected to Carrier Hall of Fame in 1995.

ROBIN M. LINDSEY
Captain, U.S. Navy
1913–1984

Premier World War II Landing Signal Officer

(LSO). From August 1941 to June 1943 he served gallantly as *Enterprise* CV-6's LSOin all, except Coral Sea, battles and strikes by U.S. Pacific carrier forces during the first 19 months of WWII. Awarded the Silver Star for the Battle of Santa Cruz 26 October 1942 "for exceptional ability and tireless devotion to duty, Lindsey minimized damage to planes of two air groups." Given a letter of commendation "for outstanding performance as LSO in *Enterprise* during the 4–6 June 1942 Battle of Midway. Received a Presidential Unit Citation and 10 battle stars. From July 1945 to September 1951 Lindsey commanded VBF-18 and VC-33. Served as *Yorktown* CV-10's Operations Officer 1954–55.

ARNOLD A. LUND
Colonel, U.S. Marine Corps
1919–1967

Korean War's premier Marine Corps carrier-based pilot. Flying from *Badoeng Strait* CVE-116, one of five Marine air group post WWII CVE-105 class carriers that saw action in Korea, Lund led his VMF-323 fighter squadron, August 1950–January 1951. In daily close action support of Marine, Army and Republic of Korea ground troops in the major battles at Pusan, Inchon, Seoul, Wonsan and Chosin Reservoir. In September VMF-323 set two carrier records, 2507 combat hours and no accidents. Lund was awarded the Silver Star and two DFCs. Citation from the commanding general of the First Marine Brigade Read: "The best close air support in the history of the Marine Corps, outstanding in its effectiveness." Elected to Carrier Hall of Fame in 1993.

WILLIAM INMAN MARTIN
Vice Admiral, U.S. Navy
1910–1996

Pioneer in carrier aviation's instrument flying, night and all-weather operations. In February 1944 from *Enterprise* CV-6, he planned the first

Vice Admiral James B. Stockdale is one of only four naval officers included in both the Medal of Honor Museum and the Yorktown Carrier Aviation Hall of Fame. USN

JAMES DAVID RAMAGE
Rear Admiral, U.S. Navy
1916–

"Jig Dog" was one of a select few to serve on carriers in three wars. During WWII he was CO of VB-10 in *Enterprise* CV-6, 1943–44. Led strikes on the Marshall's, Marianas, Truk and Palau. Won the Navy Cross for attacking carriers during the Battle of the Philippine Sea. During the Korean War he commanded Air Group 19 in *Oriskany* CV-34, 1952–54. During the Vietnam War he was awarded three Legion of Merits as Chief of Staff CTF 77 in *Kitty Hawk* CV-63 and *Constellation* CV-64, 1966–67, and ComCarDiv 7 in *Enterprise* CVN-65 and *Ranger* CV-61, 1970–72. Commanded *Independence* CV-62, 1963–64, and Naval Air Reserve, 1972–73. Elected to Carrier Hall of Fame in 1989.

DONALD E. RUNYON
Commander, U.S. Navy
1913–1984

Premier NAP, Enlisted Naval Aviation Pilot. Served with VF-6 in *Enterprise* CV-6 and VF-2 in *Lexington* CV-2 1938–42. Attached to Fighting Six in *Enterprise* June–September 1942. In supporting initial Guadalcanal invasion, Machinist Runyon on 7–8 August shot down four planes and on 24 August four more in the Battle of the Eastern Solomons becoming the first NAP ace and the top Navy F4F Wildcat ace. Awarded the Navy Cross and DFC. Promoted to Lt.j.g. September 1943. In VF-18 on *Bunker Hill* CV-17 flying F6F Hellcats, Runyon shot down three, raising his total to 11, making him the Navy's leading WWII NAP ace. From 1948 to 1951 he was Project Officer, Fighter Test Branch, Patuxent River and in 1952–53 he was CO of Fighter Squadron 22 in *Lake Champlain* CV-39. Elected to Carrier Hall of Fame in 1993.

JAMES SARGENT RUSSELL
Admiral, U.S. Navy
1903–*

Chief of Staff Carrier Division 2 during the Philippines, Iwo Jima and Okinawa invasions. Commanded *Bairoko* CVE-115, 1946–47; *Coral Sea* CV-43, 1951–53; Carrier Divisions 17 and 5, 1954–55. Chief of the Bureau of Aeronautics, 1955–57. In 1956, he was awarded the Collier Trophy along with Charles J. McCarthy for developing the first carrier-based supersonic plane, the F-8 Crusader. Vice Chief of Naval Operations, 1958–61. Elected to Carrier Hall of Fame in 1984.

CLIFTON A. F. "ZIGGY" SPRAGUE
Vice Admiral, U.S. Navy
1896–1955

Developed modern day arresting gear, 1935–37. CO of *Wasp* CV-18 from November 1943 to August 1944. Premier escort carrier (CVE) commander in the Pacific Theatre, August 1944–July 1945. As Commander Task Unit 77.4.3 "Taffy III" during landings at Leyte Gulf, he fought Japanese battleships and cruisers, Battle Off Samar, 25 October 1944. Commanded escort carrier support units during invasions of Moratai, Iwo Jima and Okinawa. Elected to Carrier Hall of Fame in 1985.

JAMES B. STOCKDALE
Vice Admiral, U.S. Navy
1923–

After nine years in a number of squadrons and at Patuxent, in 1960 he became the first pilot to log 1,000 hours in an F-8 Crusader. CO and XO of VF-51 in *Ticonderoga* CVA-14 in 1962–64. On 5 August 1964 he led the first bombing strike on North Vietnam mainland thus starting the eight year Vietnam air war. After a total of 201 strikes, two DFCs and the Legion of Merit as CAG-16 in *Oriskany* CVA-34, he was shot down 9 September 1965. After seven and a half tortuous years, he was released 17 February 1973. Awarded the Medal of Honor "For conspicuous gallantry as senior naval officer POW camps. Recognized by his captors as the leader of resistance and for refusal to participate in propaganda exploitation." Elected to Carrier Hall of Fame in 1993.

JOHN S. "JIMMY" THACH
Admiral, U.S. Navy
1905–1981

Developed "Thach Weave" fighter tactics. Led VF-3 on *Lexington* CV-2 in early 1942 and on *Yorktown* CV-5 at Midway where he became an ace by shooting down three Zeros and two torpedo planes. Admiral McCain's fast carrier Task Force 38 Operations Officer, November 1944–September 1945. Captain of *Sicily* CVE-118, 1950–51, and *Franklin D. Roosevelt* CV-42, 1953–54. Commanded anti-sub forces in the Pacific, 1957–59. Elected to Carrier Hall of Fame in 1982.

JOHN HENRY TOWERS
Admiral, U.S. Navy
1885–1955

Commissioned Naval Aviator Number 3 in 1911. Commanded *Langley* CV-1 and *Saratoga* CV-3. Chief of Staff of the Fleet's carrier force. Chief of the Bureau of Aeronautics (1939–42). During World War II Admiral Towers administered the Fleet's carriers, their Logistics and deployment as Deputy to Admiral Chester W. Nimitz. Commanded the Pacific Fleet in 1945. Elected to Carrier Hall of Fame in 1981.

FREDERICK M. "TRAP" TRAPNELL
Vice Admiral, U.S. Navy
1902–1975

Pioneer carrier aircraft test pilot. Instrumental in the development of the F6F Hellcat and the F4U Corsair, 1940–1942. Chief of Staff to Admiral Radford, Commander Carrier Division 6 aboard *Yorktown* CV-10, November 1944–August 1945. In 1949, while commanding Naval Air Test Center, Patuxent, he was given the Octave Chanute award for his work in developing carrier-based jet aircraft. Captain of the *Coral Sea* CV-43, April 1950–February 1951. Elected to Carrier Hall of Fame in 1984.

Eugene Anthony Valencia
Commander, U.S. Navy
1921–1972

Third ranked WWII Navy ace with 23 planes during two deployments with VF-9, 1943–45. Shot down seven of his total from *Essex* CV-9, three from *Lexington* CV-16, and 13 from *Yorktown* CV-10. Conceived and developed the "Mowing Machine" fighter formation aerial maneuver which his four plane division, "Valencia's Flying Circus," used to shoot down 50 planes in three months, including 14 in one mission, six by Valencia. Elected to Carrier Hall of Fame in 1983.

STANLEY W. "SWEDE" VEJTASA
Captain, U.S. Navy
1914–

One of a few WWII carrier pilots to receive Navy Crosses for dive bombing and aerial combat. With VS-5 in *Yorktown* CV-5 at Coral Sea his SBD bomb hit helped sink a carrier and his fixed guns shot down three Zeros. With VF-10 "Grim Reapers" in *Enterprise* CV-6 at Santa Cruz his F4F Wildcat in one CAP flight shot down seven dive bombers and torpedo planes saving the "Big E." Air Officer in *Essex* CV-9 during Korean War, January 1951–April 1953. Commanding officer of *Constellation* CV-64, November 1962–63. Elected to Carrier Hall of Fame in 1987.

ALEXANDER VRACIU
Commander, U.S. Navy
1918–

Fourth ranked Navy WWII ace with 19 planes. In 1943 he flew wing for five months on Medal of Honor winner "Butch" O'Hare, CO of VF-6. In *Independence* CVL-22 he got his first plane at Wake, 5 October 1943. In *Intrepid* CV-11 29 January 1944 he shot down his next three planes during the invasion of Kwajalein. On 16 February 1944 during the first ever U.S. naval forces attack on Truk, flying in the first wave, Vraciu unassisted shot down four enemy fighters. On 19 June 1944 in VF-16 aboard *Lexington* CV-16 during the Marianas Turkey Shoot, part of the Battle of the Philippine Sea, he shot down six planes in one flight. Awarded the Navy Cross. He added one more during the next day's strike on the Japanese Fleet bringing his total to 19, then a record for U.S. carrier airmen. Elected to the Carrier Hall of Fame in 1995.

JOHN CHARLES WALDRON
Lieutenant Commander, U.S. Navy
1900–1942

Dedicated skipper of Torpedo Squadron 8 who on 4 June 1942 from *Hornet* CV-8, courageously led 15 unescorted obsolete TBDs, piloted largely by USNRs who had never dropped a torpedo even in practice, in a relentless attack on the Japanese Fleet at Midway. All but one of the 30 pilots and crew perished. His and their heroism drew away enemy Zeros from U.S. dive bombers which sank three carriers. Elected to Carrier Hall of Fame in 1982.

Carrier Aviation Test Pilot Hall of Honor

ESTABLISHED WITH DEDICATION CEREMONIES on 10 October 1987, the Carrier Aviation Test Pilots Hall of Honor at Patriots Point is currently the only exhibit that honors aviators who helped build American airpower through their work as experimental test pilots of carrier-based naval aircraft. A number of pilots have made the ultimate sacrifice in this pursuit. One of them was Lt. Commander James Blackstone Taylor, Jr., USNR, for whom the exhibit is named. The Hall of Honor was created via cooperative efforts of the Museum, the Yorktown Association and James B. Taylor III. Mr. Taylor generously supported the project financially and served from its inception as coordinator of an illustrious selection panel.

Into 1998, twenty-one test pilots have been enshrined for their outstanding performance and accomplishments in the field of flight testing carrier aircraft. The text for their respective plaques is presented below.

JAMES B. TAYLOR, JR.
Lt. Commander, USNR
1897–1942

Lt. Commander Taylor learned to fly in 1914. He won his Navy wings in 1917 and began testing airplanes almost immediately. He left the Navy in 1922 and continued testing as a free lance contract pilot until his recall to active duty in 1940. He lost his life in 1942 while testing a

The Test Pilots Hall of Honor is named for Commander James B. Taylor, Jr., who was killed in 1942 while testing an experimental F4F-6 Wildcat fighter.

Navy XF4F-6 Wildcat fighter. Taylor flew 461 different aircraft during his 25-year career. Testing the most advanced Navy fighter and attack aircraft of their day, he was one of the few pilots of the 1920s and '30s qualified to perform terminal velocity dives. Lt. Commander Taylor's pioneering work paved the way for better and safer airplanes. His engineering and flying skills were a major factor in the development of a whole new technology for proving new designs. Today's sophisticated flight test operations are a living tribute to his legacy.

ERIC M. BROWN
Captain, Royal Navy
1919–

Eric Brown, recognized as Britain's foremost test pilot of carrier-based aircraft, has flown 487 different types of airplanes, including the rocket-powered German ME 163. He also is the most highly decorated test pilot veteran of the Fleet Air Arm. A World War II fighter pilot, he became Chief Naval Test Pilot at the Royal Aircraft Establishment Farnborough. On 3 December 1945, aboard the HMS *Ocean*, he made the world's first pure jet carrier landing in a DE HAVILLAND VAMPIRE MK 1. Brown's 2,407 carrier landings

and over 2,700 catapult launches are world records. His flight test work also proved new concepts in carrier operations, such as the angle deck, steam catapult and mirror landing systems. In 1951–1952 he served as a British resident test pilot at the U.S. Naval Air Test Center, Patuxent River.

MARION E. CARL
Major General, USMC
1915–1998

The Marine Corp's first World War II Ace, Marion Carl shot down 18 enemy planes—15 at Guadalcanal—and was awarded 2 Navy Crosses, 5 Distinguished Crosses and 14 Air Medals. During his initial tour, 1945–47, at Patuxent River, Carl played a vital role in early Navy investigation of jet aircraft suitability; and on 1 November 1946, became the first Marine to make a carrier landing and take-off in a jet—a modified Lockheed P-80. As Chief Test Pilot at Patuxent for all carrier-type aircraft, 1949–52, Carl did the principal carrier suitability and evaluation testing of a number of planes including the: F9F PANTER INTERCEPTOR SERIES, F2H BANSHEE INTERCEPTOR SERIES. In 1952, he was awarded the Octave Chanute Award for notable contributions to the aeronautical sciences.

*Eugene B. Ely was the first aviator to demonstrate operational use
of aircraft with naval vessels in late 1910 and early 1911.* USN

WILLIAM V. DAVIS, JR.
Vice Admiral, USN
1902–1981

A U.S. Naval Academy graduate, Bill Davis became a naval aviator in 1927. That same year he served as navigator on the winning plane in the Dole Air Race from California to Hawaii. Later he flew with the famed "Three Seahawks" and other noted Navy aerobatic demonstration teams. But his contributions to carrier aviation, beginning at Anacostia in the 1930s, far surpassed his public flying feats and in 1949 he became the second naval aviator to exceed the speed of sound flying a DOUGLAS D-558-II SKYROCKET. After service in World War II, he became Director, Flight Test at the Naval Air Test Center where he flew every type aircraft being evaluated. He also promoted the use of telemetering and photo panels to document test results. A proponent of attack helicopters, the Admiral was Deputy Commander, U.S. Atlantic Fleet, when he retired in 1960.

ROBERT M. ELDER
Captain, USN
Northrop Corporation
1918–

After earning two Navy Crosses—one at Midway—as a dive bomber pilot, Robert M. "Bob" Elder, in 1944–45, flew the first carrier trials of the F8F Bearcat and the first tricycle landing gear carrier aircraft—the FR-1 Fireball and F7F Tigercat. As Director, Flight Test Division, Patuxent, 1957–59, Elder did the first Navy development test flights on the: F-4 PHANTOM II INTERCEPTOR; A-5 VIGILANTE NUCLEAR ATTACK AIRCRAFT; F8U-3 CRUSADER III INTERCEPTOR. After retiring from the Navy in 1963, Elder spent 23 years with Northrop Corporation during which he was Director of Flight Test Operations and Chief Test Pilot. He was the driving force that applied the technologies embodied in the YF-17 into the P630 design which culminated in the highly successful F/A-18 Hornet Strike Fighter.

Commander Theodore G. Ellyson was designated Naval Aviator Number One.   USN

THEODORE G. ELLYSON
Commander, USN
1885–1928

Theodore "Spuds" Ellyson was the first naval officer assigned to receive flight training and was designated Naval Aviator No. 1. On 1 July 1911, he flew the Navy's first airplane: CURTISS A-1. Ellyson assisted in finding a way of getting short-range aircraft aloft at sea and on 7 September 1911, succeeded in taking the A-1 off from an inclined cable at Lake Keuka, N.Y. Though a crude arrangement, it was the Navy's first test of a shipboard launching devise. Following further development, Ellyson, on 12 November 1912, made the first successful catapult launching at the Washington Navy Yard on the Potomac River piloting the new CURTISS A-3. For this important test the Navy used a compressed air system based on its torpedo launches. "Spuds" also was the first Navy pilot to fly at night and was with the Fleet in World War I.

EUGENE BURTON ELY
1886–1911

Eugene B. "Gene" Ely, a civilian member of the newly formed Curtiss Exhibition Company, was the first aviator to demonstrate the operational use of aircraft with naval vessels—taking off and landing on a ship. On 14 November 1910 Ely flew a 50-hp CURTISS PUSHER from a wooden ramp rigged over the bow of the cruiser USS *Birmingham*, resting at anchor in Hampton Roads, Va. Then, on 18 January 1911, flying the same Curtiss Pusher, Ely landed on and took off from a similar platform built on the stern of the battleship USS *Pennsylvania* anchored in San Francisco Bay. These feats marked the beginning of carrier aviation. For the trials on the *Pennsylvania*, Ely and the Navy had devised an arresting gear not unlike that of a modern carrier. Lines were stretched between sandbags across the battleship's make-shift "flight deck." The lines snagged hooks under the plane, enabling it to land short.

*William V.
Davis, Jr., (later
Vice Admiral),
left, and Daniel
W. Tomlinson
(later Captain,
USNR), flew
with the "Three
Seahawks" in
1927. Both are
honored in the
Test Pilots Hall
of Honor.*   USN

DONALD D. ENGEN
Vice Admiral, USN
1924–

Donald "Don" Engen enlisted in the Navy at 18
and rose to the rank of Vice Admiral. He retired
in 1978 as Deputy Commander-in-Chief, U.S.
Atlantic Command and U.S. Atlantic Fleet. An
engineering test pilot in both the U.S. and the
United Kingdom, Engen has flown over 250 different types of aircraft. He has performed spin
tests on most Navy tactical models and flew the
first shipboard trials on mirror landing systems.
He also flew development and evaluation tests
on such Navy jets as: F4H-1 PHANTOM IN-
TERCEPTOR; F8U-3 CRUSADER INTERCEP-
TOR; A3J-1 VIGILANTE ATTACK BOMBER.
Engen was a dive bomber pilot in World War II
and fighter pilot in Korea. He received the Navy
Cross for his role in sinking a Japanese carrier
in the 1944 Battle of Leyte Gulf. Long a propo-

nent of air safety, Don also served his country
with distinction on The National Transportation
Safety Board and as Administrator of the Fed-
eral Aviation Administration.

LAWRENCE E. FLINT
Captain, USN
1920–

Experimental flight tests performed by Larry Flint
in both U.S. and British aircraft have contributed
much toward the advancement of naval carrier
aviation. After flying fighters in World War II,
Larry flew tests on the F7F, F8F and F4U series at
Patuxent River. In 1957 he spearheaded efforts
to make high performance carrier jets more speed
stable and control responsive on glide slopes, using the F8U-2 Crusader for most of the test work.
In 1959 he set a world altitude record of 98,560
feet in a McDONNELL F4H PHANTOM II. Also

*Donald D. Engen (later Vice Admiral) flew development and evaluation tests
on the F4H-1 Phantom, F8U-3 Crusader and A3J-1 Vigilante.* USN

with the F4H, Flint pioneered shipboard trials of new concepts in night lighting. Through clever innovation, his group developed an all-new flight deck lighting system that gave carriers "around-the-clock" capability. Today night carrier operations, though still challenging, are almost routine. Larry is an SETP associate fellow.

ROBERT L. HALL
Vice President, Grumman Aircraft Corporation
1905–

An aeronautical engineer and experimental test pilot, Robert "Bob" Hall had 10years of aircraft development experience when he joined Grumman in 1936. Also a former race pilot, he designed and flew the famous "GeeBee" racing plane.Hall helped design the fighters and bombers that contributed so much toward winning the war in the Pacific. Among his first test flights

were the following Grumman aircraft: XTBF AVENGER TORPEDO BOMBER, XF6F-1 HELLCAT FIGHTER, XF7F-1 TIGERCAT NIGHT FIGHTER, and the XF8F-1 BEARCAT FIGHTER.

As Chief Engineer, he was also responsible for the design of two outstanding Grumman carrier jet fighters of the Korean War, the straight-wing F9F Panther and swept-wing F9F Cougar. Bob became Vice President in 1954. He is a fellow of the American Institute of Aeronautics and Astronautics and an honorary fellow, Society of Experimental Test Pilots.

CORWIN H. MEYER
Grumman Aircraft Engineering
1920–

"Corky" Meyer began flying in 1937. He joined Grumman as an experimental test pilot in 1942.

Lt. James L. Pearce, USN, shot down six Japanese planes before becoming a test pilot at Naval Test Center, Patuxent River, in 1946. He is shown here in front of an FJ Fury. USN

JAMES L. PEARCE
Lieutenant, USN
North American Aviation Company
1919–

After shooting down six Japanese planes during deployments, 1943–1945, in fighter squadrons aboard *Bunker Hill* C17 and *Hornet* CV-12, James "Jim" Pearce, in 1946, became an experimental test pilot at Naval Test Center, Patuxent River. Retiring from the Navy in 1948, Pearce joined North American Aviation as an experimental and engineering pilot. During 1950–61 he was Chief Test Pilot and Manager Engineering Test of N.A.'s Columbus, Ohio, Division. Among the many planes at Patuxent and North American for which Pearce did the principal testing were the first jet fighters to be carrier based, the FJ FURY INTERCEPTOR SERIES and the attack bombers which gave the Navy's carrier arm the atomic bomb capabilities of the Air Force's new B-36, the AJ SAVAGE NUCLEAR ATTACK BOMBER SERIES.

FORREST S. PETERSEN
Vice Admiral, USN
1922–1990

Forrest "Pete" Petersen graduated from the Naval Academy in June 1942 and became a naval aviator in 1944. After flying fighters and earning an aeronautical engineering degree he was assigned to the Naval Air Test Center, Patuxent River where he instructed test pilots and helped prove most of the new carrier-based fighters of that era such as the F11F TIGER FIGHTER, F8U CRUSADER INTERCEPTOR, and the F4H PHANTOM 11 INTERCEPTOR.

As the Navy's test pilot on the program, Petersen flew the initial research flights of the famous X-15 experimental rocket plane at Edwards AFB. Later he commanded *Enterprise* CVN-65, the Navy's first nuclear carrier. Under his leadership while commanding the Naval Air Systems Command, the F/A-18 Hornet, AV-88 Harrier and LAMPS Mark 111 Seahawk made

In 1954 he became history's first civilian test pilot to qualify aboard a U.S. Navy aircraft carrier with a jet airplane. As project pilot, he tested Grumman F6F, F7F, F8F and most of the world's competitive fighters, including the Japanese Zero. In 1947 he flew Grumman's first jet, the GRUMMAN XF9F-2 PANTHER. He was also the only pilot assigned to fly the prototype Grumman XF10F-1 Jaguar, the first variable geometry plane designed for production. While its operational problems halted the project, his year-long flight testing proved invaluable in advancing swept-wing aircraft development. When Corky retired in 1978, he was president and CEO of Grumman American aviation, a subsidiary firm. He is a founding member of SETP and a former consultant to NASA.

Forrest S. Petersen (later Vice Admiral) flew the experimental X-15 and later commanded the nuclear carrier Enterprise *(CVN-65). USN*

their successful first flights. "Pete" was a longtime Fellow of the Society of Experimental Test Pilots and the American Institute of Aeronautics and Astronautics.

ROBERT O. RAHN
Captain, USAAF
Douglas Aircraft Company
1920–1998

After 103 WWII combat missions flying Spitfires in the European Theatre, Robert "Bob" Rahn graduated from the USAAF's second test pilot class and became an experimental test pilot at Wright Field. In late 1945 Rahn joined Douglas (later McDonnell Douglas) as an engineering test pilot, and over the next 11 years did the first flight, development, spin, etc., tests on a number of planes including the AD SKYRAIDER ATTACK AIRCRAFT, F4D SKYRAY INTERCEPTOR, and A4D SKYHAWK ATTACK AIRCRAFT.

Testing the Skyraiders, 1945–49, Rahn set an unofficial world record for payload (bombs, rockets, etc.) at 10,000 lbs. In 1953 the Skyray piloted by Bob became the first carrier aircraft capable of Mach 1.0 in level flight and to hold a world speed record.

CHARLES A. "CHUCK" SEWELL
Lieutenant Colonel, USMC
Grumman Aerospace Corporation
1930–1986

After 110 combat missions in Korea and 220 missions over Vietnam and four years at Naval Air Test Center, Patuxent River, Chuck Sewell retired from the Marine Corps and joined Grumman in 1969 as an experimental test pilot. In 1971 he was promoted to Chief Test Pilot and in 1974 named Deputy Director, Flight Test. During Sewell's 17 years with Grumman he did the principal experimental testing of the following outstanding operational carrier aircraft: A-6, A-6B, A-6D and A-6E INTRUDERS, and the F-14A TOMCAT.

In 1985, acknowledged as the free world's best experimental test pilot, he conducted the first flight and initial envelope expansion of the forward-sweep X-29. Winner of the 1974 Octave Chanute Award from the American Institute of Aeronautics. Winner in 1973 and 1983 of the Society of Experimental Test Pilots Kincheloe Award as the Test Pilot of the Year. Sewell is only the second pilot to win this prestigious honor twice.

ROBERT K. SMYTH
Grumman Aerospace Corporation
1927–

Bob Smyth served 10 years in the U.S. Navy, including over three years flying fighters, such as the F8F, F4U and F2H. He graduated from the Navy Test Pilot School in 1952 and was first assigned to its Electronics Test Division. As a member of the USN/Royal Navy exchange program, Smyth helped form the Royal Navy's first night fighter squadron. He joined Grumman in 1955, becoming chief test pilot in 1967 and director of flight test in 1974. Bob performed "first flights" on several new jets, notably the A-64 INTRUDER LONG-RANGE STRIKE AIRCRAFT, and the F-14A TOMCAT AIR SUPERIORITY FIGHTER.

His experimental work at Grumman also included structural, spin and carrier suitability tests on the F9F Cougar and F11F Tiger series. Besides test flying, Bob also served as consulting pilot for Grumman's pioneering Lunar Lander program. He is an associate fellow of SETP.

Captain Robert M. Elder, USN, Ret., earned two Navy Crosses in World War II before moving to Patuxent as Director, Flight Test Division in 1957. USN

APOLLO SOUCEK
Vice Admiral, USN
1897–1955

A Naval Academy graduate, Apollo Soucek won his Navy wings in 1924. Soon he was testing both early carrier aircraft and sea planes. In 1930 he set a new world altitude record of 43,166 feet in an experimental Pratt & Whitney-powered WRIGHT F3W APACHE. For pioneering the Navy's high altitude flight experiments, Soucek received the Distinguished Flying Cross. Later he served in *Lexington* CV-2, *Saratoga* CV-3, *Ranger* CV-4 and *Yorktown* CV-5. Soucek was *Hornet* CV-8's air officer when the historic "Doolittle Raid" was launched against Tokyo in 1942, and executive officer when the ship was sunk. He was highly decorated for valiant leadership in WWII and Korea. Soucek became Commander, Naval Air Test Center, Patuxent, in 1947; and Chief of the Bureau of Aeronautics in 1953. In both posts he guided the development and evaluation of some of the Navy's newest and most advanced weapon systems.

W. PAUL THAYER
Chance Vought Aircraft
(United Aircraft/LTV Corporation)
1919–

A U.S. Navy combat ace in World War II, Paul Thayer flew fighters in both European and Pacific theaters where he earned numerous decorations for valor. He joined Chance Vought in 1948 and soon became the first civilian experimental test pilot to graduate from the Navy Test Pilot School. He flew a variety of carrier jets and performed critical tests on such types as the XF6U-1 PIRATE (VOUGHT'S FIRST JET FIGHTER), and the XF7U-1 CUTLESS TWIN-JET FIGHTER.

Flying an XF7U-1, he became the first pilot to break the sound barrier in a Navy fighter. He was also the first pilot to use a Navy ejection seat in an emergency. In 1982 Paul resigned as chairman and CEO of LTV to accept a presi-dential appointment as Deputy Secretary of Defense, where he again served his country with distinction. He is the recipient of many awards and is a fellow of SETP.

FREDERICK M TRAPNELL
Vice Admiral, USN
1902–1975

For the period 1930–1950, Frederick "Trap" Trapnell was universally regarded as the Navy's foremost test pilot. As a project test pilot at the Flight Test Section, Anacostia, 1930–32, Trapnell tested many prototype carrier aircraft including Grumman's XFF-1, Curtiss' F8C and Vought's O3U. Returning to Anacostia, 1940–42, to head the Flight Test Center, "Trap" did the principal tests on the Navy's premier World War II fighter planes, the GRUMMAN F6F HELLCAT, and the VOUGHT F4U CORSAIR.

In 1949–50, while commanding the Naval Air Test Center, Patuxent, Trapnell did the first Navy evaluation testing of the XF9F-2 Panther, XFJ-1 Fury, XF2H-2 Banshee and XF-7U-1 Corsair and won the 1949 Octave Chanute award for his work in developing carrier based jet aircraft.

DANIEL W. TOMLINSON
Captain, USNR
1897–1995

Daniel W. "Tommy" Tomlinson graduated from the U.S. Naval Academy in 1917. He served as an observer on anti-submarine patrol during World War I and subsequently won his wings as Naval Aviator No. 2923. Tommy's distinguished flying career covered every element of naval aviation, including Chief of Flight Tests at NAS ANACOSTIA. He also formed and led the "Three Seahawks," the Navy's first precision aerobatic team, flying the BOEING F2B-1 CARRIER-BASED FIGHTER. His pioneering work in the fields of experimental flight test, air combat strategies, high altitude research and all-

*Richard M. Wenzell served combat tours in World War II and Korea
before and after serving as a test pilot.* USN

weather flying contributed significantly to military and commercial aviation. Many advances in air transport technology were the direct result of his innovations. An expert on air logistics in World War II, Tommy retired in 1951. He became an honorary Fellow of SETP in 1988.

RICHARD M. WENZELL
*North American Aviation
(Rockwell International)
1922–1986*

After flying fighters and torpedo planes against submarines in the Atlantic during World War II, Richard "Dick" Wenzell was the top graduate (1948) in the Navy Test Pilot School's first class at the Naval Air Test Center, Patuxent River. Wenzell also flew fighters in Korea. He was then assigned to NATC until joining North American Aviation (later Rockwell International) in 1953. At NAA he performed initial flight program structural and aerodynamic tests as well as carrier suitability trials on North American jets, including the FJ-4 FURY INTERCEPTOR SERIES, and the A-5 VIGILANTE ATTACK BOMBER.

Dick served as NAA's Chief Test Pilot, Flight Test Manager and ultimately Director of Flight Operations and Logistics. His many decorations include the Distinguished Flying Cross, Air Medal with four Gold stars and a Presidential Unit Citation. He was a Fellow in the Society of Experimental Test Pilots.

1987 charter inductees

THE 1987 CHARTER INDUCTEES were Carl, Elder, Ellyson, Ely, Pearce, Rahn, Sewell, Trapnell and Taylor. In 1990 Hall, Engen, Soucek and Wenzell were enshrined. Petersen was inducted in 1991; Flint, Smyth and Thayer in 1993; and Brown, Davis, Meyer and Tomlinson in 1995.

Admiral George "Gus" Kinnear, USN, Ret., stands with the family of the late Lt. Col. Charles A. Sewell, USMC, during his induction into the Test Pilots Hall of Honor, October 1987. YORKTOWN ASSOCIATION

The Test Pilot Hall of Honor was originally placed on the second deck of *Yorktown*, but was later moved to Hangar Bay I. Immediately above the Hall of Honor is a full scale replica of the 1903 Wright Brothers Flyer, the aircraft that made the first powered, sustained and controlled flight. Built and donated by the Charleston-based Robert Bosch Corporation, the replica was dedicated on 17 December 1993, the 90th anniversary of the famous event.

Scheduled for induction in October 1998 are Rear Admiral E.L. "Whitey" Feightner, USN, Ret., Admiral John T. Hyland, USN, Ret., and Edward T. Schneider.

Enlisted Combat Aircrew Roll of Honor

THE NAVAL AVIATION Enlisted Combat Aircrew Roll of Honor was established by proclamation aboard *Yorktown* on 10 October 1996. The Roll of Honor recognizes enlisted aircrew of the Navy, Marine Corps and Coast Guard who have distinguished themselves in combat. The first and only inductee on 10 October 1996 was radioman-gunner Bruno Gaido from Air Group Six aboard *Enterprise* (CV-6). Gaido, also the only enlisted man honored in the Yorktown Carrier Aviation Hall of Fame, received the Distinguished Flying Cross posthumously after he was killed following the June 1942 Battle of Midway. On 11 November 1997 the following were inducted into the Roll of Honor.

George Bobb
Benno F. Brandt
James J. Brennan
Allen Brost
Leo H. Burrows
Joseph Caracappa
David J. Cawley

Clarence L. Christensen
John E. Clark
Wayne C. Colley
Nick Cooney
William H. Cromell
Edmond R. Danis
Raymond J. Dansereau
Otis Dennis
Richmond R. Emery
William T. Estes
Harry H. Ferrier
John D. Floyd
Charles G. Fries, Jr.
William J. Gerbe
James M. Geyton
Robert L. Giuliani
Michael M. Glasser
Sherwin H. Goodman
Robert W. Gruebel
Mark A. Hardisty
Wesley R. Hargrove
Harold F. Heard
Eugene G. Herkins
Harvey Herzog
Earl E. Howell
Arthur C. Hurrell
Harry R. Jespersen
Jenus B. Jones
Charles E. Kateliner
Alvin Kernan
Adolph W. Kolodzik
Arthur A. Kopta
John F. Leonard
William J. Martin
Stuart J. Mason
Donald P. Meyer
William C. Miller
John W. Montgomery
Robert M. Phillips
Thomas A. Powell
Joseph S. Price
Kenneth W. Rocheblave
Carl B. Schilligo
Richard T. Schoonover
Melvin R. Schultz
Lawrence C. Shepherd

Charles E. Shineman
Alfred R. Smith
Irwin M. Smith
Raymond G. St. Pierre
Rudolph Valasek
Thomas T. Watts
Stanley N. Whitby
Delmer D. Wiley
Jerry T. Williams

NAVY PATROL SQUADRON 22, CREW 7

(Daniel J. Ballenger, Ronald A. Beahm, Cecil H. Brown, Clifford R. Byers, Roy Ludena, Robert L. French, William F. McClure, Robert L. McDonald and Lloyd Smith). Coast Guard Air Sea Rescue (Joseph R. Bridge, Winfred J. Hamond, Robert F. Hewitt, J.M. Miller, Tracy W. Miller and Carl R. Tornell)

Inducted 9 October 1998

Adkins, Floyd D.
Aiken, Vernard V.
Anderson, Herbert C.
Arcidiacono, Pancrazio F.
Austin, Eugene V.
Babcock, Ellis C.
Bailey, Lewis C.
Baron, Edwin A.
Bennie, John A.
Bihun, Nick
Blackwell, Leland P.
Bonner, John P.
Brodeur, Robert J.
Bruce, Thomas J.
Brunetti, Anthony W.
Carnazza, Vincent C.
Cashmore, William E.
Childers, Lloyd F.
Clarkson, Robert E.
Clausen, Jr., Raymond M.
Cohen, Walter E.
Day, Joseph N.
Deceuster, Ralph J.

Deptula-Drew, Walter J.
Dewey, John L.
Dixon, Philip M.
Dockter, Wilbert W.
Doktor, Robert A.
Edinger, James C.
Eley, Henry W.
Ferrara, Mario
Fisher, James J.
Flack, Roger M.
Fordham, Robert J.
Forshee, Lynn R.
Frierson, Walter D.
Gallagher, Robert T.
Gentzkow, Richard F.
Glass, Jack
Globus, Leonard J.
Guthrie, Harry H.
Hale, William F.
Hall, Meda R.
Hammond, Robert N.
Harrison, Morse G.
Hays, Robert V.
Heard, Harold F.
Hoff, Donald L.
Horton, LaVerne C.
Hughes, Calvin R.
Irwin, Edgar G.
Jocks, Donald B.
Kissick, James W.
Kozlesky, Joseph K.
Leaming, Jack
Mayer, Clyde V.
McLemore, Winston
McMullin, Joseph F.
Mercer, Larry B.
Merritt, Thomas E.
Miller, Robert C.
Molleston, Robert D.
Monnett, Donald R.
Moore, Oral L.
Nadison, Steve
Nelson, Thomas C.
Nulty, Emmett H.
Orr, John J.
Oubre, John B.

Oubre, John A.
Parker, Alva J.
Pelletier, Lionel F.
Rhodes, Duane L.
Richards, Wallace B.
Richardson, Charles J.
Rowell, Edwin O.
Schmeeckle, Willis M.
Schroeder, Vernon E.
Sennett, Walter M.
Shaffer, Frederick S.
Sheehan, Paul H.
Shuttleworth, Frank
Smith, Duncan C.
Smythe, Milton C.
Snowden, John W.
Stanley, Howard T.
Thornton, Len C.
Tiffany, Earl C.
Ufer, Frank E.
Wall, Clarence T.
Wareing, John
Wilkinson, Richard T.
Wilson, Eudora B.
Zorbach, Anthony J.

PATROL BOMBER SQUADRON 25 CREW 8

(Frederick C. Barnes, Warren H. Daley, Donald H. Douglas, Thomas J. McGowan, Joseph N. Venditti, Gordon H. Yates, Vincent M. Grady, and Charles L. Hamilton)

TORPEDO SQUADRON 8

USS *Hornet* (CV-8)
(Ross E. Bibb, Jr., Robert K. Huntington, Ronald J. Fisher, George A. Field, Horace F. Dobbs, Otway D. Creasy, Jr., Darwin L. Clark, Max A. Calkins, Amelio Maffei, Hollis Martin, Tom H. Pettry, Bernard P. Phelps, Aswell L. Picou, Francis S. Polson, and William F. Sawhill)

All Killed in Action at Midway, 4 June 1942

The Naval Aviation Enlisted Combat Aircrew Roll of Honor recognizes enlisted aircrew of the Navy, Marine Corps and Coast Guard who distinguished themselves in combat. Seen here is Henry W. Eley, a highly decorated "back-seat" gunner who manned his guns on combat flights in both the SBD Dauntless and SB2C Helldiver. USN

TORPEDO SQUADRON 8 (Detached)

Nelson L. Carr,* Arnold T. Meuers,* Arthur R. Osborne,* Charles E. Fair,* Howard W. Pitt,* William C. Lawe,* James D. Manning,* Lyonal J. Orgeron,* John W. Mehltretter,* and Harry H. Ferrier)

Killed in Action at Midway, 4 June 1998

TORPEDO SQUADRON 3

USS *Yorktown* (CV-5)
(Troy L. Barkley,* Robert B. Brazier,* John R. Cole,* Raymond J. Darce,* William A. Phillips,* Leo E. Perry,* Charles L. Moore,* Joseph C. Mandeville,* Harold C. Lundy,* Richard M.

Hanson,* Benjamin R. Dodson, Jr.,* and Lloyd C. Childers)

Killed in Action at Midway, 4 June 1942

TORPEDO SQUADRON 6

USS *Enterprise* (CV-6)

(John H. Bates,* John M. Blundell,* Gregory J. Durawa,* Edwin J. Mushiniski,* Harold F. Littlefield,* Arthur R. Lindgren,* John U. Lane,* Charles T. Grenat,* Wilburn F. Glenn,* D.L. Ritchey, W.C. Humphrey, W.D. Horton, W.N. McCoy, and D.M. Cossitt)

Killed in Action at Midway, 4 June 1942

3

Remembrance of the Ships
of Patriots Point

USS Yorktown (CV-10)

USS *Yorktown* (CV-10) is the tenth aircraft carrier to serve in the United States Navy ("CV" is the designation for large, fast aircraft carriers). She was named for the first carrier *Yorktown* (CV-5) that was lost while helping repel the Japanese during the Battle of Midway in June 1942. One of the first members of the new Essex class, CV-10 joined 20 other large fast carriers (CVs) and nine fast light carriers (CVLs) of the Independence class to participate significantly in the Pacific offensive that began in late 1943 and ended with the defeat of Japan in 1945. *Yorktown* received the Presidential Unit Citation (the highest award for a U.S. Navy ship) and 11 battle stars for World War II action, arrived off Korea too late for combat but later earned five battle stars for service off Vietnam.

Construction

Yorktown (CV-10), the fourth U.S. Navy ship to bear the name, was laid down on 1 December 1941 at the Newport News Shipbuilding & Drydock Company. Originally named *Bon Homme Richard*, the hull was renamed *Yorktown* on 26 September 1942 to honor the recently lost *Yorktown* (CV-5). Although the Essex class design was inspired by the CV-5 class, the new carriers were over 8,000 tons heavier with a standard displacement of 27,100 tons. Fully loaded with ordnance, fuel, aircraft and supplies for both ship and crew, displacement ranged up to 36,000 tons. Overall length was originally 872 feet, over 50 feet longer than CV-5, while the beam was 93 feet at the waterline and 147 feet, six inches across the flight deck (83 feet and 110 feet for CV-5). Maximum draft was just over 28 feet and top speed was near 33 knots, specifications quite similar to the older *Yorktown*. Designed to accommodate 2,600 officers and men including air groups, over 3,400 crowded into the ship during World War II. For endurance, the new *Yorktown* was designed to travel 20,000 miles at 15 knots: the old *Yorktown* was designed to steam 12,000 miles at the same speed. Perhaps the most significant difference in the design of the two carriers was the internal arrangement of the boiler rooms and engine rooms. If the first *Yorktown* had the alternating boiler-engine room arrangement, most likely she would have survived the Battle of Midway.

For striking power the new *Yorktown* could comfortably carry 90 planes, usually 36 fighters, 36 dive bombers and 18 torpedo bombers. *Yorktown* CV-5's design aircraft complement was 72 planes. For defense against aircraft targets within four miles, the new *Yorktown* carried 12 five-inch dual purpose .38 caliber guns plus 32 40mm and 46 20mm guns.

In response to the critical need for new fast carriers to replace the four fast carriers lost in 1942 and to support the Pacific offensive, construction was rushed to complete CV-10 and her

*Two views of the
USS Yorktown
(CV-10) in
World War II
configuration.*
USN, USN

Captain J.J. "Jocko" Clark (later Admiral), first commanding officer of Yorktown
*(CV-10), inspects the ordnance gang in 1943. At his left is Lt. j.g. James T. Bryan,
Jr., who founded the Yorktown Association in 1948 and led
that reunion group for nearly 50 years.* USN

sister ships. Whereas CV-5 required nearly four years to build during the peacetime Depression years, the new *Yorktown* was built in only 14 months. On 21 January 1943 CV-10 was launched and christened by Mrs. Eleanor Roosevelt who had served as sponsor for the first *Yorktown*. Eager to get into combat, the new *Yorktown* started down the ways' moments before expected and the president's wife had to seize the champagne bottle and quickly smash it against the hull. Less than three months later, *Yorktown* was commissioned on 15 April 1943 at the Norfolk Navy Yard.

World War II History

WITH CAPTAIN Joseph J. ("Jocko") Clark in command, the new carrier remained in the Norfolk area until 21 May 1943 at which time she got underway for shakedown training near Trinidad. During this time *Yorktown* was used by Hollywood for filming what would become the 1944 Academy Award winning documentary motion picture "The Fighting Lady," a nickname that has remained with the ship. Just as he had before the commissioning of the ship, Captain Clark adamantly drove his officers and men toward the goal of perfection. Most of the officers were newly commissioned reserves. They and the young, inexperienced crew had little or no naval frame of reference and probably thought all commanding officers were as tough and efficient as Jocko Clark. Only later would they appreciate his competence and understand that the hard work he demanded was intended not only to defeat the Japanese but also to save their lives

The new carrier returned to Norfolk on 17 June 1943 and continued air operations. Commanding officer of the carrier's first air group

(Air Group 5) was fighter ace Commander James H. Flatley, Jr. Flatley had distinguished himself in combat in the May 1942 Battle of the Coral Sea flying from the first *Yorktown* and later as commanding officer of Fighting 10's "Grim Reapers" flying from *Enterprise* (CV-6) during the critical battles off Guadalcanal. Now, it was his responsibility to form and train the new air group for combat.

On 6 July 1943 *Yorktown* began her journey to the Pacific Ocean transiting the Panama Canal on 11–12 July and arriving in Pearl Harbor on 24 July. Following a month of training exercises, *Yorktown* , as part of Task Force 15 with new carriers *Essex* (CV-9) and *Independence* (CVL-22), steamed toward her first combat operation. On 31 August 1943 the carrier launched fighter and bomber strikes against Marcus Island. Although not remembered as one of the major Pacific battles, the Marcus raid was significant for testing air operations in a multi-carrier formation and for introducing the new Essex class and Independence class carriers and F6F Hellcat fighter to combat.

In early September 1943 *Yorktown* made a quick round trip to San Francisco for aircraft and supplies and then prepared for combat. On 5 October the carrier's planes began two days of raids against Wake Island, one of many assaults against the island that had been lost early in the war despite the valiant resistance of U.S. Marines.

On 10 November *Yorktown* departed Pearl

Lt. j.g. Richard "Dick" Tripp, Landing Signal Officer (LSO) for much of CV-10's World War II combat tours, guides a plane to the carrier's deck. USN

Harbor with Task Force 50 to participate in her first major assault operation, the occupation of Tarawa, Abemama and Makin in the Gilbert Islands. On 19 November the carrier launched raids to suppress enemy airpower in the Marshall Islands (Jaluit and Mili) several hundred miles north of the Gilbert Islands. Next day Air Group Five planes were active over both the Marshalls and Gilberts. Before retiring to Pearl Harbor on 9 December, the carrier's planes raided installations on Wotje and Kwajalein Atolls in the Marshall's.

Following a month of training, on 16 January 1944 *Yorktown* joined the fast carriers again for another amphibious assault, Operation "Flintlock." This time the Marshall Islands would be occupied. As part of Task Group 58.1 on 29 January (a task force is comprised of task groups) with *Lexington* (CV-16) and *Cowpens* (CVL-25), Air Group Five flew strikes against Taroa airfield on Maloelap Atoll. The following day the target was Kwajalein and beginning on the 31st until 4 February the pilots aim was even more precise as they few in support of the invading troops.

Following the Marshall Islands occupation, Captain Clark was promoted to Rear Admiral and Captain Ralph E. Jennings assumed command of "The Fighting Lady." With new carriers, new air groups, men and supplies becoming available at a steady pace, the offensive across the Pacific accelerated in 1944. For the next several months *Yorktown* was constantly at sea engaging in a series of raids against Japanese island strongholds. With the capture of Majuro in the Marshall Islands, replenishment time was considerably reduced. On 16–17 February 1944 *Yorktown*, in company with other carriers and surface units built around several of the new fast battleships, struck hard and successfully against Truk Atoll in the Caroline Islands, the Japanese Navy's most important forward base. Before all the fires were out at Truk, Rear Admiral Marc A. Mitscher led the fast carrier task force further west for the first raids against Saipan in the Mariana Islands (22 February). On 30–31 March the target was enemy installations in the Palau Islands.

On 13 April *Yorktown* headed with her task group for the northern coast of New Guinea. On 21 April she began launching raids in support of General Douglas MacArthur's assault on Hollandia, beginning with attacks in the Wakde-Sarmi area. On 22 April Air Group Five began providing direct support to the landing areas at Hollandia. This was followed by another raid on Truk lagoon on 29–30 April.

In early Mary 1944 *Yorktown* was again at Pearl Harbor, but on this occasion she was there for more than replenishment. Air Group Five was transferred off with Air Group One coming aboard. Following two weeks of training operations near Hawaii, the big carrier headed back to Majuro, arriving in time for the next major operation. Although *Yorktown* would end the war with 11 battle stars, none would be more significant than the one she earned in the forthcoming 19–20 June 1944 Battle of the Philippine Sea, often remembered as "The Marianas Turkey Shoot." The goal of the operation was to occupy Saipan, Tinian, and Guam. The loss of these islands had considerable impact upon Japan. The Japanese cabinet headed by Tojo, who had brought Japan into the war, was dismissed. Further, Japan now came within reach of the new, long range Army Air Force B-29s. On the American side, there was considerable satisfaction in reclaiming Guam which had been overrun and lost in the first days of the war.

Pilots of Air Group Five enjoy a light moment in a CV-10 ready room. USN

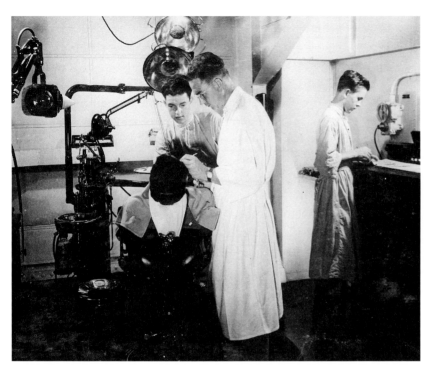

Truly a "floating city," Yorktown offered the services found in most small towns and cities. The Dental Quarters aboard CV-10 appear today as they did from the ship's operational days. USN

Aboard *Yorktown*, primary consideration was to air operations. Once discovered, there was no question that the Japanese would commit her carriers and all available air power to stop the American advance. Air Group One first struck Guam (11–13 June) followed by a raid to the north to hit targets in the Bonin Islands (16 June). By 18 June it was known that enemy planes were moving into position to challenge the U.S. Navy both from land bases and from carriers. On the morning of 19 June Air Group One was over Guam to destroy land based aircraft, and before noon first indications appeared that Japanese carrier planes were heading toward the American task force. Air Group One torpedo-bombers and dive bombers continued strikes on Guam while the Hellcat fighters moved to intercept the incoming enemy attack. *Yorktown* planes claimed 37 of the nearly 400 lost by the Japanese in the two day battle.

Operational orders required the task force commander, VADM Raymond Spruance, to first secure control of the air and sea for the invasion forces. Consequently, finding and pursuing the Japanese carriers was delayed. Indeed, when the order of battle was formulated, no one on either side expected the American aerial victory to be so overwhelming. Late on 20 June, the fleeing Japanese task force was sighted heading west toward safety. Along with other carriers, *Yorktown* began launching at 1623 (4:23 PM) and about 1840 the enemy force was attacked. The Japanese lost only one carrier in this attack, that loss (*Hiyo*) credited to the air group flying from *Belleau Wood* (CVL-24). *Yorktown* pilots made several hits but recorded no sinkings. Arriving back over their task force after dark, Air Group One pilots—like those from other carriers—landed on whatever deck they could find. Of the six major carrier verses carrier battles in the Pacific, the Battle of the Philippine Sea was the only one in which "The Fighting Lady" participated, but her air groups and ships company gave an excellent account of themselves. (The six major carrier battles were Coral Sea, Midway, Eastern Solomons and Santa Cruz, all in 1942, Battle of the Philippine Sea and Leyte Gulf, both in 1944.)

Unable to catch and complete the destruction of the enemy carrier force, the fast carriers returned to continue support of the landings in the Marianas and to attack installations in the Bonins, including a 24 June strike against Iwo Jima. Except for replenishment retirements (which would soon be available at Ulithi, an excellent anchorage in the Caroline Islands just south of the Marianas), *Yorktown* continued strikes in and around the Marianas until the end of July when she steamed back to the United States. Arriving in Puget Sound Navy Yard at Bremerton, Washington, on 17 August 1944, she then underwent a two month overhaul. While the overhaul proceeded, a catapult was added to the portside of the flight deck, the hangar bay catapult was removed and the entire exterior of the carrier was painted in a "dazzle" camouflage design to confuse the enemy as to speed and direction.

While the overhaul was needed and the pilots and crew were happy to be back in the United States, the timing precluded *Yorktown* from participating in the decisive 25–26 October 1944 Battle of Leyte Gulf. Still, there were significant battles to be fought, and in early November she was back with the fast carriers ready for more combat. New to the carrier was her third commanding officer, Captain Thomas S. Combs and her third air group, Air Group Three.

Although *Yorktown* had missed the just concluded major sea battle, occupation of the Philippines would require several months and "The Fighting Lady" would contribute to the eventual victory. Beginning 7 November 1944 Air Group Three planes struck targets in the Philippines in support of the Leyte invasion (central Philippines), and in December continued the pounding in preparation for landings on Luzon (northernmost major island in the Philippines).

On 17–18 December *Yorktown* endured the infamous typhoon that sank three USN destroyers and assisted in the rescue of survivors from those ships. Returning to combat 3 January, Air Group Three hit airfields on Formosa (northwest of Luzon) and in the Philippines to provide support for American troops during the Lingayen Gulf landings on the west coast of Luzon.

Beginning on 12 January 1945 the fast carriers entered the South China Sea for anti-shipping attacks and strikes on Indochina (Vietnam), southern China and Hong Kong. Leaving that area, strikes were made against Formosa and Okinawa before returning to Ulithi at the end of the month. On 16 February planes from *Yorktown* and other fast carriers were active in support of the invasion and occupation of Iwo Jima, a volcanic island in the Bonins approximately halfway between the B-29 air bases in the Marianas and the Japanese mainland. On the 16th and 17th Air Group Three's targets were airfields around Tokyo, not only to destroy enemy aircraft but to prevent them from moving

Seriously hit by a Japanese bomb only once, smoke rises from that 18 March 1945 attack in this view. Detonation occurred near the compartments currently used for executive offices.
USN

to defend Iwo Jima. From 20–23 February *Yorktown* planes flew missions in direct support of the landings and then returned to strike the Japanese homeland. These strikes continued until the end of February when the carrier again returned to Ulithi.

Before returning to action, *Yorktown* took aboard the fourth of the five different air groups to fly from her deck during World War II. Air Group Nine reported 6 March 1945 and stayed aboard until 17 June. Although aboard for a relatively short time, Air Group Nine nonetheless scored impressive numbers in downing enemy planes. The primary reason for the high score was that the period from March through May 1945 was the height of the kamikaze attacks on U.S. naval forces, primarily those around Okinawa. A number of the Japanese suicide pilots lacked adequate training, and that fact plus the inability of their bomb laden planes to make necessary evasive maneuvers contributed to their heavy losses.

On 14 March *Yorktown* steamed west to resume raids on Japan and to begin support work for the Okinawa invasion scheduled for 1 April. On 18 March while Air Group Nine was flying missions against the enemy homeland, the carrier was attacked several times. After near misses, a bomb hit the carrier's signal bridge, traveled down the starboard side through 20mm gun battery number seven and exploded outboard of the second deck in the area presently utilized for the World War II Fast Carrier Exhibit. The explosion resulted in the death of five men, left two dozen wounded, and left two large holes in the starboard side. The carrier's guns shot down

Pilots render honors for one of their own on Yorktown's *port side elevator, June 1944.* USN

the enemy plane that dropped the bomb and "The Fighting Lady" remained fully operational, continuing missions against Japan proper. Currently on display in the World War II Fast Carrier Exhibit on *Yorktown's* hangar deck, one can view a shackle attached to the Japanese bomb that survived the 18 March 1944 explosion. It was found within feet of the area where it is currently displayed.

On 21 March *Yorktown* steamed for Okinawa and began air strikes on the 23rd, and except for a short return for strikes against the Japanese mainland, most of her operations for the next two months were in support of the battle for Okinawa. In this time the carrier was constantly alert for air attacks, and her crew saw several kamikaze hits against other ships in her formation. However, *Yorktown* continued to be a lucky ship in evading kamikazes, thanks in no small part to the effectiveness of her anti-aircraft gun crews. Still, several kamikazes missed CV-10 by only a few feet.

Air attacks off Okinawa proved a constant threat, but just as memorable was the one occasion when it appeared the major threat would be an encounter with the remaining Japanese super-battleship, *Yamato*. On 7 April *Yamato* and other enemy warships were discovered heading for Okinawa. Only the Japanese knew that their ships were headed on a suicide mission to beach themselves on Okinawa and fight to the end. The enemy plan came to nothing, however, as planes from *Yorktown* and other carriers in-

tercepted the formation well short of Okinawa. Air Group Nine and other air groups registered hits. Additionally, AG-9 contributed bombs and torpedoes that sank the light cruiser *Yahagi*.

Soon after the destruction of *Yamato*, on 23 April 1945 Captain Combs was relieved by Captain Frederick Boone who remained on the bridge through the remainder of the Okinawa campaign and the final strikes of the war against the Japanese homeland. On 17 June Air Group 88 relieved Air Group Nine, and flew numerous missions over Japan, including the last dogfight, before Japan agreed to end the fighting on 15 August. Air Group 88 helped cover the occupation landings in late August and early September, and air-dropped supplies to Allied prisoner-of-war camps. Although the crew enjoyed the great fly-over during the formal surrender on 2

Flight deck crew work to remove a crashed jet on 9 April 1953. Yorktown *arrived off Korea just after the June 1953 truce.* USN

Greatly altered in appearance after modernization in 1955, Yorktown *today
is basically unchanged from that date.* USN

September, they also marked 16 September 1945 as a special day to remember. On that day *Yorktown* dropped anchor in Tokyo Bay. Her long, hard fought voyage from Newport News was indeed over.

Mothballs, Modernization, The Cold War and Vietnam

IN THE FIRST MONTHS after World War II, *Yorktown* participated as a unit of the "Magic Carpet" fleet returning servicemen from Pacific bases to the United States. Bunks were installed on the carrier's hangar deck, and other changes were made to accommodate the veterans. Round-trip voyages were made to Guam and the Philippines transporting nearly 10,000 passengers. By 1 February 1946 the ship was in Seattle, Washington, where she awaited inactivation overhaul. Decommissioned there 9 February 1947, the carrier was placed in the Bremerton

Group, U.S. Pacific Reserve Fleet, where she remained until the Korean War.

The need for the carrier's return to active service became apparent soon after the June 1950 Communist invasion of South Korea. Entering the Puget Sound Naval Shipyard in June 1952 she underwent modernization overhaul (Project SCB-27A). When recommissioned 15 December 1952 she had a more streamlined island configuration, the 5-inch guns fore and aft of the island were removed, 3-inch guns replaced the older 40mm guns, the 20mm were moved ashore, and a new escalator was installed. These changes were the most visible, but less visible changes were equally significant. Aircraft the *Yorktown* would now serve were larger and faster (jets were quickly replacing WWII era prop planes), consequently a stronger flight deck was required. Elevators needed to be larger and stronger, catapults required greater capacity, and greater fuel storage was required both for aircraft and the ship itself. *Yorktown* steamed to the Far East in

August 1953 and became flagship of Fast Carrier Task Force 77. The July 1953 armistice in Korea was holding and the ship saw no combat.

Off San Francisco in the spring of 1954 "The Fighting Lady" starred in another movie, "Jet Carrier." By July, however, she was in the Far East, and when the Nationalist Chinese evacuated the Tachen Islands to Taiwan in January and February 1955, *Yorktown* provided air cover.

Back at Puget Sound Naval Shipyard in March 1955, the carrier underwent her second major modernization overhaul, Project SCB-125. Before returning to sea in October 1955, *Yorktown* received an angled flight deck, an enclosed bow, and improved living quarters for both officers and men. Gone were the 3-inch gun sponsons immediately beneath the island.

In late 1956 installation of a mirror-light landing system was added to the attack carrier (CVA), and in September 1957 she received the last major visible change to her silhouette. While being refitted for her new role as an antisubmarine warfare aircraft carrier (CVS-10 effective 1 September 1957), the number three elevator was moved outboard on the starboard side. Since becoming a museum, the starboard deck-edge elevator has served as the main entrance for visitors.

Yorktown began her service as an antisubmarine carrier in earnest after completing her overhaul in February 1958, still operating in the Pacific. While the Soviet Union in the 1950s did not pose a surface threat to the U.S. Navy, her submarine force did have considerable potential. Air groups on *Yorktown* and other antisubmarine carriers needed to search out Soviet submarines in any weather, day or night. Instead of dive bombers and torpedo planes, *Yorktown* now carried helicopters and fixed-wing S-2 "Tracker" and E-1 "Tracer" planes equipped with ever-improving radar. In case of war, electronic rockets, homing torpedoes, and depth charges were aboard. Several fighter aircraft were aboard in case of air attack. Additionally, *Yorktown* had the capability to escort convoys and provide close air support for amphibious assault. While it never became necessary to use her radar and weapons during the Cold War, her search planes played a

A Yorktown Recipe

Recipes, such as the one here for cookies, required huge storage and preparation areas. Refrigeration was a problem during World War II, but veterans recall the quality and quantity of food as "very good."

10,000 Chocolate Chip Cookies

112 Pounds of Chocolate Chips
165 Pounds of Flour
500 Eggs
100 Pounds of Granulated Sugar
87 Pounds of Shortening
75 Pounds of Brown Sugar
12 Pounds of Butter
3 Pounds of Salt
3 Cups of Vanilla Extract
1 Quart of Water
1.5 Pounds Of Baking Soda

significant role in the rescue of 52 merchant seamen from a British freighter that ran aground during a typhoon 10 June 1960.

The possibility of combat operations became readily apparent in late 1958 and early 1959 when the carrier participated in an American show of strength in response to the communist Chinese shelling of Quemoy and Matsu, small offshore islands held by the Nationalist Chinese. Immediately thereafter, the carrier steamed to the waters off Vietnam in response to internal disorder. Soon, internal disorder became open warfare in Vietnam, and in 1964 and 1965 *Yorktown* was operating continuously off that country providing antisubmarine protection for the attack carriers. On "Yankee Station" in 1966 the carrier's fixed wing planes provided direct air support to land operations. Throughout the early years of the Vietnam War, *Yorktown* was involved in search and rescue missions.

In February 1967 *Yorktown* underwent her last major overhaul as part of the Fleet Rehabilitation and Modernization program (FRAM). This program was intended to extend the useful

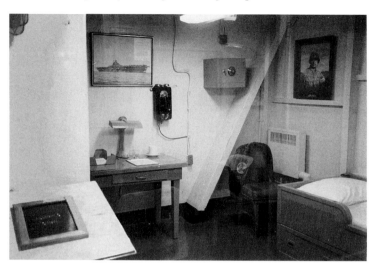

The Flag Officer's in-port stateroom is located abeam and to port of the Captain's in-port quarters.

life of a ship and *Yorktown*, like many of her WWII-era sister ships, was showing her age. Although a pipe might look sound from the outside, corrosion on the inside not only could make it nonfunctional but also could make it dangerous. Electronics needed replacing more often because of improved technology rather than aging, and new functions of the ship and equipment quickly expanded beyond the available space on the Essex class carriers. Before her FRAM was completed in October 1967 a decision was made to decommission "The Fighting Lady" within three years. Consequently, not all the improvements planned for her FRAM were implemented.

In 1968 *Yorktown* again served off Vietnam. Late that year, she again starred in a movie, this time standing in for the first *Yorktown* (CV-5), *Enterprise* (CV-6) and *Hornet* (CV-8) and even Japanese carriers. The movie, "Tora! Tora! Tora!" recreated the Japanese attack on Pearl Harbor. Released in 1970, the movie has become a classic for students of World War II as the screenplay remained true to historical facts. Perhaps the two best views of *Yorktown* are during takeoffs of the Japanese planes, especially the overhead shots as the planes depart for Pearl Harbor, and

Yorktown Association Wardroom Exhibit on the second deck. Significant memorabilia are displayed in cases on top of former officer wardroom dinning tables.

Photographs of Yorktown's *commanding officers surround the painting of CV-10's first CO, Capt. J.J. Clark, in the James T. Bryan, Jr., Lounge located just aft of the Wardroom.*

Captain's Cabin, in-port quarters showing desk and four-place mess table. Usually, the CO dined alone.

near the end of the movie when the carrier enters Pearl Harbor (portraying *Enterprise*).

After the movie filming, *Yorktown* served as a recovery ship for the Apollo 8 space shot which was the first manned flight to circle the moon and return. Astronauts Frank Borman, James Lovell and William Anders were picked up by helicopter and landed aboard the carrier on 27 December 1968.

The final assignment for *Yorktown* carried her back to the place of her birth. On 28 February 1969 the carrier joined the Atlantic Fleet at Norfolk, Virginia. Operations and visits to Europe concluded her active service and on 27 June 1970 the ship was decommissioned at Philadelphia as part of the Atlantic Reserve Fleet. On 1 June 1973 she was struck from the Navy list and was later moved to Bayonne, New Jersey, scheduled to be her last port before being scrapped. Acquired by the Patriots Point Development Authority in 1974, the carrier was towed to Charleston Harbor in June 1975, and formally dedicated as a memorial on 13 October 1975 as part of the 200th anniversary of the Navy.

Yorktown Wardroom

AFTER THE *Yorktown* arrived at Patriots Point, veterans of the carrier selected the Officer's Wardroom and an adjacent ready room for the display of their memorabilia. The space utilized by the Yorktown Association is divided into three display areas: the James T. Bryan, Jr., Lounge; the Wardroom, and the CVA/CVS-10 Room.

The James T. Bryan, Jr., Lounge is named in honor of the founder and longtime executive director of the Yorktown Association. After serving with distinction as an aviation ordnance officer aboard *Yorktown* from her commissioning, Bryan returned to his New York home and business on Wall Street after the war. Remaining in the Naval Reserve, he rose to the rank of Commander. In 1948 he organized the first reunion

Commanding Officer's in-port stateroom.

for the veterans of the "Fighting Lady" at Ruppert's Brewery in New York City. When news was announced that the *Yorktown* was to be scrapped after her 1970 decommissioning, Bryan led the Yorktown Association in its successful bid to join with officials in South Carolina to bring the carrier to Charleston Harbor. Over the years, Jim Bryan led countless fund raising campaigns to assist with the procurement of aircraft and preservation of the ship. Further, he initiated plans for the National Memorial to Carrier Aviation ("Arlington"), the Carrier Avia-

tion Hall of Fame, the Test Pilot's Hall of Honor, memorial plaques for pilots and aircrew lost from *Yorktown*, and a host of other programs. A dedicated, tireless advocate and entrepreneur on behalf of the U.S. Navy, naval aviation and the Yorktown Association, Commander Bryan suffered a debilitating stroke on 7 December 1996. Current and future generations will be educated to a significant portion of American history that most likely would have been overlooked without the contributions of "Mr. Yorktown" over a period of 50 years.

Within the James T. Bryan, Jr., Lounge is a large painting of Mr. Bryan, pictures of other CV-10 veterans who have devoted much of their time and resources to the Yorktown Association; pictures of all 26 commanding officers of the *Yorktown*; a display of books and booklets pertaining to CV-10; and

Flag Officer's in-port mess. In the large picture on the bulkhead, President Harry S Truman is seen dining in the Admiral's mess aboard the Franklin D. Roosevelt *(CV-42).*

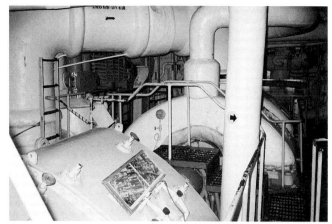

Engine rooms deep in Yorktown's *hull. During World War II the carrier could reach a top speed of 33 knots, but it dropped to 30 knots after modernization.*

numerous displays featuring annual reunion highlights from 1948 through 1995. Since 1948 most of the greats of naval aviation have been special guests, either for induction into one of the honor programs or simply to enjoy the annual festivities.

The Wardroom is reserved for the World War II *Yorktown* veterans to display memorabilia, and to remember several who earned a special place of honor. Upon entering the Wardroom, a visitor will find a ten foot model of the carrier as she appeared in camouflage paint in late 1944. Paintings, photographs, newspaper and magazine articles chronicle the 1943-1945 years of the carrier's life. Memorabilia offered for display includes uniform parts, the 1943 commissioning pennant, a portion of the homeward bound pennant, landing signal officer paddles and numerous paper items. Medals, swords, uniform parts, citations and other paper items were donated by the families of the World War II commanding officers J.J. Clark, Ralph E. Jennings, Thomas S. Combs and W.F. Boone, all of whom later rose to flag rank. Also remembered with paintings are Rev. Robert L. Alexander and Father Joseph

N. Moody, chaplain's during World War II.

In addition to the commanding officers, memorabilia is displayed in honor and memory of several notables. Medals (Navy Cross, Distinguished Service Cross, Legion of Merit, Distinguished Flying Cross and Air Medal, among others), pictures and paper items recall the life and contributions of Vice Admiral James H. Flatley, Jr., who made the first landing aboard *Yorktown* in 1943 and served as the carrier's first air group commander (CAG-5). Pictures and ci-

The machine shop appears today as it did when Yorktown *was decommissioned in 1970. When at sea, repairs occasionally required the manufacture of new parts.*

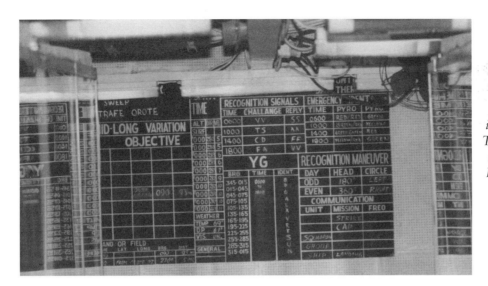

Ready room information boards. This one is located in the Air Group One Ready Room on the gallery deck.

tations recall the lives of Commander Charles Crommelin, the carrier's second CAG, and his brother, Richard, who won a Navy Cross for the Battle of the Coral Sea and another for the Battle of Midway before losing his life off *Yorktown* as Fighting Squadron 88's commanding officer. After World War II the U.S. Navy honored Clark, Flatley and the Crommelins' by naming Oliver Hazard Perry-class guided missile frigates in their honor (FFG-11, FFG-21 and FFG-37, respectively).

Veterans of the *Yorktown* remember Lt. Elisha Terrill "Smokey" Stover not only as a fearless fighter pilot but also as a sensitive, young lover of poetry and of life. Memory of his tragic loss inspired many of the memorials extant aboard *Yorktown*. In the Wardroom are photographs of "Smokey," along with his cold weather flight jacket and the letter he left addressed "To whoever is unlucky enough to have to inventory my belongings."

Lt. (later Rear Admiral) James W. "Pop" Condit was shot down and captured during the carrier's first action in August 1943. Released from a POW camp in Japan, he was summoned to the battleship *Missouri* on 2 September 1945 to represent naval aviator POWs during the surrender ceremony. On display in the Wardroom is his surrender certification, post cards he sent from the POW camp and a sword he obtained from one of his Japanese guards when released.

Although not located in the Wardroom, four other displays are extensions of its theme to honor veterans of the carrier. On the flight deck, portside aft, is a small display dedicated to the memory of Lt. "Dick" Tripp, one of the more outstanding landing signal officers during World War II. A second display, located off the flight deck immediately inside the island is the Aviation Ordnance Memorial Armory in honor of Joseph Coppi, AOM2c, USNR, a rearming crew chief who was killed in a flight deck plane

Combat Information Center on Yorktown.

While no longer open for business, the Soda Fountain was Yorktown's *most popular compartment when the ship was in service.*

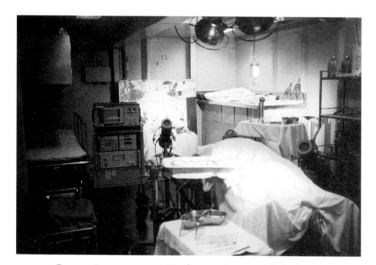

Operating room on Yorktown's *second deck.*

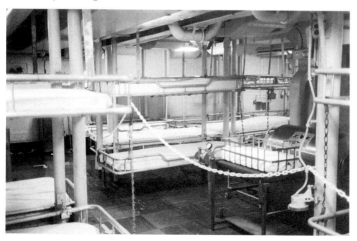

Sick bay bunks on Yorktown's *second deck.*

crash and fire on 23 November 1943. A third exhibit on the gallery deck is a large display in honor of Air Group One. A pilot's ready room is configured as it was originally while the adjoining compartment, originally an enlisted aircrew ready room, displays over a hundred pictures depicting not only pilot's but also scenes they recorded during the war. Both compartments display flight suits and other flight gear as well as status boards and briefing notes.

The fourth display is mounted on the front wall ("wall" instead of "bulkhead" as it was never part of the ship) of the Smokey Stover Memorial Theatre. Some 20 bronze plaques pay honor to notables who served aboard the carrier. Plaques dedicated by the end of 1997 include:

In memory of Lt. E.T. "Smokey" Stover, lost after the first strike on Truk, February 1944;

In memory of Commander Eugene A. Valencia (1921–1972), leading ace aboard *Yorktown* and third ranking U.S. Navy ace with 23 kills;

Chief Petty Officer's (CPO) mess. These compartments are currently used to feed over 15,000 overnight campers each year as well as lunch for the visiting public.

In memory of Commander Charles Crommelin (1909–1945), second commanding officer of Air Group Five;

In memory of Vice Admiral James H. Flatley (1906–1958), first Air Group Commander aboard *Yorktown*;

In memory of Commander Donald Richard Hubbs, commanding officer of VS-23, lost off North Vietnam 17 March 1968;

In memory of Captain Walter Franklin Henry (1911–1991), commanding officer of Torpedo Squadron One;

In memory of Ensign Owen H. Ramey and his Torpedo Squadron Five crewmen Doyle D. Parker and James M. Russell;

In memory of Lt.j.g. Carl H. Sanborn and his Torpedo Squadron One crewmen James E. Buchanan and Earl J. Steffen;

In memory of Vice Admiral Ralph E. Jennings, second commanding officer of *Yorktown*:

In memory of Vice Admiral Thomas S. Combs (1898–1963), third commanding officer of *Yorktown*;

In memory of 13 squadron-mates lost in 1944 from Fighting Squadron One;

In memory of nine pilots lost from Fighting Squadron 88;

In memory of 11 squadron-mates lost from Bombing Squadron Five;

In memory of 10 squadron-mates lost from Fighting Squadron Five;

In memory of 18 squadron-mates lost from Fighting Squadron Three;

In memory of 16 squadron-mates lost from Air Group Nine;

In memory of 10 ship's company lost in action aboard *Yorktown*, five on 23 November 1943 and five on 18 March 1945;

In memory of Edward Steichen (1879–1973), in charge of Naval aerial photography during World War II;

In memory of James D. Sparks (1910–1987), Torpedo Squadron One gunnery officer; and

In honor of Robert L. Alexander, first Protestant chaplain aboard *Yorktown*.

The Yorktown CVA/CVS-10 Room was once used as a ready room, but was transformed into a display area to depict the history of the carrier from the 1950s until decommissioning. Photographs, many enlargements from *Yorktown* cruise books, paintings, memorabilia, and the union jack hauled down during the 27 June 1970 decommissioning ceremony are displayed.

Captain and Flag Officer's In-Port Quarters

DURING THE 15 April 1993 *Yorktown* 50th Anniversary celebration, the restored Captain and Flag Officer's in-port quarters were opened to the public. Since the arrival of the carrier in 1975, these spaces were used as administrative offices for the Patriots Point staff. Renovation began in 1992 and the spaces were restored to give visitors a feel for the many years of use (1943–1969) rather

The brig was Yorktown's *most unpopular compartment when the ship was operational. Requests by current staff to reactivate the brig to house some overnight campers have been consistently rejected by higher authority.*

Marine quarters aboard Yorktown. *The marines were responsible for shipboard security and served anti-aircraft batteries during World War II.*

than attempting to restore to one specific year or war period.

The renovation was generously funded by former commanding officer Captain James B. Cain. During World War II, Cain flew F6F Hellcats from the *San Jacinto* (CVL-30) and returned from the Pacific war as an ace with 8.5 kills. Later he served two combat tours flying jets during the Korean War. From June 1965 through May 1966 he commanded the *Yorktown* off Vietnam. Among his many decorations on display in the restored Captain's Cabin are the Silver Star, Legion of Merit, four Distinguished Flying Crosses

and 13 Air Medals. Captain Cain also donated photographs and paintings from his career and time aboard *Yorktown* along with several pistols, rifles, a shotgun and uniforms.

Displayed in the Captain's Cabin are renderings by the late Joe Cason of all 25 *Yorktown* commanding officers. Also displayed are photographs of the 12 March 1966 Ann-Margret Show aboard *Yorktown*, the Captain's desk, and mess table with place settings for four even though the commanding officer usually dined alone. Visitors can view the Publications Office, Linen Locker and Head (bathroom) as well as the Captain's Pantry. The Captain's Stateroom displays period uniforms, bed and furniture.

Immediately to port from the Captain's Office are the Flag (Admiral's) Quarters. Open for viewing are the Flag Pantry; the Flag Office with World War II era telephone and desk lamp plus a 1946 Philco radio-record player; the Admiral's Cabin with shower; and the Flag Mess with conference table set for nine. A large picture depicts the Flag Mess aboard the newly commissioned carrier *Franklin D. Roosevelt* (CV-42) in October 1945. At the head of the table is Admiral Marc Mitscher with President Harry Truman immediately to his right and Secretary of the Navy James V. Forrestal to his left.

USS Laffey (DD-724) in post World War II configuration, but before the major modifications of the 1962 FRAM overhaul. Among significant changes from World War II shown in this view are missing torpedo tubes (just forward of the aft 5 inch gun mount) and the enclosed bridge (immediately aft of the number two 5 inch gun mount). USN

THE WOOD FLIGHT DECK

THROUGHOUT THE HISTORY of aircraft carriers, flight decks have been either wood or steel. During World War II, the British opted for steel decks because they operated in close proximity to the European continent and expected to absorb heavy damage. However, in choosing a steel flight deck, the British gave up speed and size of their air groups (to remain within prewar treaty limits).

The United States in World War II used flight decks of wood, mostly Douglas Fir three to four inches thick, with only a thin sheet of steel beneath the wood to stop water and serve as a fire break. Wood was much lighter and enabled U.S. Navy carriers to operate at high speed across the vast Pacific. Too, the U.S. Navy was willing to accept battle damage to the flight deck as it was relatively easy to repair. The hangar deck of all U.S. carriers was steel with

the intent of stopping battle damage at that level. Further, the light steel sides of the hangar bay were designed to vent damage out and up. The British design was to stop bombs on the flight deck. Any bomb penetrating to the hangar deck would have caused extensive structural damage well beyond what could usually be expected to an American carrier.

Battle experience in World War II demonstrated that both Britain and the United States had chosen the best designs for their overall needs. Still, near the end of the Pacific war, Japanese kamikazes caused far greater damage to American carriers than to British steel deck carriers. Such experience along with larger and faster aircraft led the U.S. Navy to develop steel deck carriers, beginning with the Midway class and continuing on in the design of the later super-carriers of the 1950s to the present.

USS LAFFEY (DD-724)

WITH A Presidential Unit Citation, five battle stars for World War II and two for the Korean War, the *Laffey* (DD-724) is the most decorated World War II era destroyer still in existence. DD-724 inherited her name from the first *Laffey* (DD-459) which was sunk on the night of 13 November 1942 during the fierce Naval Battle of Guadalcanal. The Bristol class DD-459 was also awarded a Presidential Unit Citation and received three battle stars.

Port side view of Laffey *at her new pier at Patriots Point. Much of the destroyer's underwater hull was replaced and the hull painted in 1995.*

Both DD-459 and DD-724 were named in honor of Seaman Bartlett Laffey (1841–1901) who was awarded the Medal of Honor for heroism during the Civil War. At Yazoo City, Mississippi, on 5 March 1864, Seaman Laffey landed a 12 pound howitzer with its crew during a battle and helped repulse a heavy Confederate assault.

Laffey (DD-724) was laid down 28 June 1943 by Bath Iron Works Corporation, Bath, Maine, and launched 21 November 1943. The new destroyer was sponsored by Miss Beatrice F. Laffey, daughter of Seaman Laffey, and was commissioned 8 February 1944 with Commander F. Julian Becton in command.

The new *Laffey*, an Allen M. Sumner class destroyer, displaced more tonnage, was longer and possessed heavier armament than her predecessor. DD-724 displaced 2,200 tons, was 376 feet, six inches long with a 41 foot, one inch beam, and she was fitted with six 5-inch guns in three twin mounts (DD-459 carried four 5-inch guns in single mounts). *Laffey* carried six 21 inch torpedo tubes and intermediate range 40mm (12 barrels in two twin mounts and two quad mounts) and eleven single mount 20mm guns. At 34 knots, the new *Laffey* was not as fast as DD-459 which had a top speed of 37.5 knots. Complement for DD-724 was 336 officers and men; DD-459 carried 210.

Completing shakedown, *Laffey* steamed to Bermuda and then returned to Norfolk where she served as a school ship. In May she headed for New York to join the screen of a convoy escort for England. In England, *Laffey* prepared for the invasion of France. On 3 June she headed for the Normandy beaches escorting landing craft. The group arrived off "Utah" beach at dawn on D-Day, 6 June 1944. On 6–7 June *Laffey* screened to seaward and on 8–9 June she bombarded gun emplacements. Replenishing at Plymouth, the destroyer returned to the coast of Normandy. On 12 June DD-724 pursued enemy "E" (patrol) boats which had torpedoed the destroyer NELSON. *Laffey* broke up their formation and prevented further attacks. On 25 June DD-724 joined Bombardment Group 2 shelling defenses at Cherbourg, France. Two destroyers were hit in this engagement and *Laffey* took one hit that did little damage. On 4 July *Laffey* steamed with Destroyer Division 119 for Boston. After overhaul, DD-724 sailed to Norfolk.

On 26 August *Laffey* departed for Pearl Harbor. On 23 October after extensive training, she steamed for the war zone via Eniwetok and Ulithi. Joining the screen of Task Force 38 on 5 November 1944, which was then conducting air strikes against enemy shipping, aircraft, and air-

These two photographs depict battle damage to Laffey *on 16 April 1945 that resulted in 103 casualties.*
USN

fields in the Philippines, *Laffey* served as escort and plane guard for the carriers. On 7 December *Laffey* covered landings at Ormoc Bay, silenced a shore battery and shelled Japanese troop concentrations. With Close Support Group 77.3 *Laffey* supported landings for Mindoro 15 December, and in January 1945 she screened amphibious ships landing troops in the Lingayen Gulf area of Luzon. In February *Laffey* supported Task Force 58 which struck targets in and around Tokyo before moving to take and occupy Iwo Jima.

In March 1945 *Laffey* sailed with the task force for the Okinawa invasion and helped capture Kerama Retto. Assigned to a radar picket station north of Okinawa— the most likely approach for Japanese kamikazes—the destroyer endured her most traumatic moments on 16 April 1945 which left her with

103 casualties (see Sidebar for battle details). Towed from the battle area and then ordered to Seattle, *Laffey* was still undergoing repairs when the Pacific war ended. Immediately after the war, DD-724 operated in Hawaiian waters until 21

May 1946 when she participated in the atomic bomb tests at Bikini. On 17 June 1947, *Laffey* was decommissioned and placed in reserve.

On 26 January 1951 *Laffey* was recommissioned with a former executive officer, Commander Charles Holovak, in command. After shakedown out of San Diego, the destroyer, now carrying 3-inch anti-aircraft guns in place of her 40mm and 20mm guns, steamed for Norfolk, which would be her home port for most of her remaining operational life. In March 1952 *Laffey* arrived off the coast of Korea and operated with Task Force 77 screening carriers and providing bombardment support. By late August, the destroyer was back at Norfolk, and for the next two years she operated with a hunter-killer anti-submarine group, primarily in the Caribbean. In late 1956 DD-724 served in the Mediterranean during the Suez crisis.

Continuing patrols in the Atlantic, Mediterranean and Caribbean, the destroyer underwent a Fleet Rehabilitation and Modernization (FRAM) overhaul in 1962 which raised her displacement to over 2,500 tons and markedly changed her configuration amidships. The most noticeable change was the addition of a helicopter hangar and landing pad for DASH helicopters (see Aircraft section for details of the drone antisubmarine helicopter). Returning to duty in the same antisubmarine role, *Laffey* remained in frontline service until 1970 when she was ordered to the Naval Reserve as a training ship at Alexandria, Virginia. Decommissioned 29 March 1975, she was used as a test ship for electromagnetic radiation before being transferred to the Patriots Point Development Authority in August 1978. In August 1981 the famous destroyer was towed to her berth at Patriots Point and opened to the public in the spring of 1982.

Text-plates, pictures and models help interpret the function of destroyers in the Laffey's *main deck World War II Destroyer Exhibit. Another compartment immediately aft lists the honors and sacrifice of World War II destroyers.*

Shipboard Exhibits

THE MAJOR EXHIBIT, of course, is the *Laffey*. Visitors find the five inch mounts in their original locations, and these guns and the bridge are the favorite attractions. Much of the interior of the ship is presented as though the destroyer was still in commission. The most significant change since final decommissioning was the removal of the amidships berthing compartments to make room for the World War II Destroyer Exhibit (see).

Like the *Yorktown* and *Clamagore*, *Laffey* veterans have a compartment to present their mementos. Aboard *Laffey*, the mess deck remains the domain of the destroyer's veterans. Some donations call remembrance to the first *Laffey* (DD-459), others emphasize DD-724's World War II or Korean War service.

Perhaps the most poignant exhibit is a compartment forward on the main deck that has been converted to a memorial for all killed on both destroyers named *Laffey*. Large paintings, Presidential Unit Citation plaques and wreaths direct attention to the ultimate sacrifice made aboard both ships.

USS LAFFEY AND A PLACE CALLED OKINAWA

(This article by the author was originally published in Sea History, *Spring 1995, and is reprinted here with modifications.)*

IN THE LATE SUMMER of 1944, 336 young men, most of whom were only months out of high school, stood on the main deck of the USS *Laffey* (DD-724) as she passed through the Panama Canal from the Atlantic and Caribbean to the Pacific Ocean. Admiring the beauty of the Canal Zone and marveling at the impressive engineering of the canal, some thought they would someday experience the satisfaction of telling their future children and grandchildren they had participated in the D-Day invasion of Normandy, which their ship had come through a few months before. Little else, they then thought, could equal such a story. For nearly one third of the crew, however, it was just as well that the future could not be known.

In the early spring of 1945, *Laffey* headed with hundreds of other ships to a place called Okinawa. Most of their crews had no trouble with the island's pronunciation but few had much idea where it was. All knew it was close to Japan; only a few had sufficient knowledge to cause apprehension. In Japan, of course, people knew well where Okinawa was, only 350 miles from the Japanese homeland. They knew the people of the island, they knew that many friends and acquaintances were serving there in uniform, and they knew the significance of the impending battle. Since the fall of the Marianas in the summer of 1944, the Japanese government could not keep from the Japanese people that the war they had launched three years before with the attack on Pearl Harbor was being lost. B-29 bomber raids on the home islands had become commonplace. The loss of Okinawa would mean even more air raids, and the big island could serve as a staging area for invasion of the sacred homeland itself. It would also sever shipping lanes to South Pacific raw materials and island garrisons. For the men of the approaching United States Fleet, this was expected to be just another invasion, larger but probably similar to Iwo Jima a few weeks earlier, where nearly all the opposition was ashore and the ships offshore incurred little damage from Japanese shore batteries.

For all Japanese there were no illusions as to what this battle meant: a foothold for an invasion of the homeland must not be gained. Every desperate measure necessary would be taken to prevent the fall of Okinawa.

The Japanese resolve to defend Okinawa was backed by some sound military thinking which had sometimes been lacking in previous battles. Ashore, troops dug intricate tunnels well away from the beach areas to lessen the telling gunfire effect of U.S. battleships, cruisers, destroyers and even auxiliaries. Into the tunnels went tons of supplies and 130,000 men mentally prepared to fight for soil that was Japanese in culture. Remnants of the Japanese surface navy, now without benefit of a viable carrier force for either attack or defense, fueled and armed for engagement. Airmen, both Army and Navy, utilized what little fuel reserves remained to train other pilots to get their planes off the ground and navigate to the waters off Okinawa. Little emphasis was placed on landing as these pilots were to fly only one way, and by using the most effective guidance system extant—the human mind—crash-land themselves with their bombs on the decks of American ships. If enough ships could be sunk or damaged, perhaps American public opinion would pressure politicians to deem the price of victory too high, and the United States would be willing to negotiate a peace leaving Japan unoccupied and with at least some of her empire intact.

The usual softening-up prelude in late March was contested but went well, and when ground forces were landed on 1 April, there was no significant Japanese resistance. Moving inland, things changed dramatically and it was soon apparent that the well-entrenched Japanese would have to be exterminated yard by yard, body by body. At sea, kamikaze planes and Japanese surface units became more active. Overprotected for most of her life, the giant Japanese super-battleship *Yamato* was fueled for a one-way voyage to beach herself on the shores of Okinawa and use her 18-inch guns to repel the invader. Far short of her objective, she was caught in the open sea and sunk by planes from Task Force 58—some from the *Yorktown*, a carrier which today is on exhibit with the *Laffey*.

BEFORE THE CAMPAIGN for Okinawa was over, nearly 5,000 sailors were dead, the chief instrument of Japanese destruction being the kamikaze. While many of the kamikaze pilots demonstrated a lack of training by missing their sea targets by only feet, others wrought havoc. Not all kamikazes were poorly trained: documents found on the bodies of some pilots indicated they were well trained, even flight leaders. A 550kg bomb could do considerable damage by itself, but when it slammed into a ship, the blast and fire usually ignited other flammables such as ordnance, oil, paint, wood and mattresses. Suicide attacks against battleships usually did little damage to the vessel, but took a severe toll of anti-aircraft gunners. Against destroyers, bombs were extremely lethal as the thin plating and narrow beam left little margin of safety for the ships where speed was their first line of defense. Any hit on the engines was likely to be fatal since loss of power meant insufficient capacity to remove water or fight fire.

Destroyers were exceedingly vulnerable off Okinawa since they were used as pickets—ships set out on the periphery of the fleet to help detect enemy planes flying too low to be picked up on radar. Being the first American ship sighted, and appearing from the air to be an easier target than one protected by thousands of anti-aircraft guns from a concentrated for-

mation, destroyers were favored as kamikaze targets. In addition, picket ship destruction helped eliminate the communications system to the more desired targets, the aircraft carriers. And, as in earlier battles off Guadalcanal, tying ships to a restricted area deprived them of the mobility essential for the defense of naval units. The price for violating this naval axiom—even though necessary—was the loss of 15 U.S. Navy warships of which 12 were destroyers or smaller destroyer escorts.

The kamikaze attacks caused *Laffey's* crew to experience feelings of many other sailors during that time, amounting to a state of anomie—a loss of norms, loss of knowledge of one's place and purpose in the war. The rules of war seemed to change: where one used to have a fighting chance of survival by dodging an attacker or shooting him down at high altitude, now ships were being hit by pilots who aimed their planes directly at the targets without thought for their own survival. There were no more nervous jokes to U.S. pilots to let one enemy plane come through "so we'll have something to shoot at." To many American sailors it no longer seemed a question of whether or not they would die, but when.

Such attitudes disappeared for the men of the *Laffey* on 16 April 1945. That morning there would be no time for fear or to ponder anomie: there was only time to fight. Even though the battle off Okinawa was only days old, the crew of the *Laffey* fully understood that in battle one must be totally focused on killing the foe: any other attitude would mean sure death. Focused, calm but cursing, from the ship's captain, Commander F. Julian Becton, to the most junior rating several decks below, the men of the *Laffey* stood by the guns and at battle stations to meet the enemy planes low on the horizon. At a range of over four miles, the six 5-inch guns on the racing destroyer opened up, their proximity fused shells bouncing the attackers. At a little over a mile the 40mm guns, mostly in twin mounts, began their rhythmic discharge and at 800 yards the 20mm guns began their staccato barking. For the next hour and ten minutes there would be no time to think, only time to act and react. For 32 men it would be their time to meet death.

ABATTLE IS FOUGHT as much with the brain as with brawn. Fully exposed to both enemy and his own ship's ordnance, Commander Becton raced the bridge, spotting the several kamikazes in their final dives and ordering the helmsman to turn hard to port or starboard as the moment demanded. One plane that appeared to have taken perfect aim could not compensate for Becton's last-second maneuver: it carried away a portion of the mast before striking the water beside the ship, splattering plane and bomb parts against *Laffey*, wounding several men but killing only fish. Another radical maneuver at the last second spoiled the aim of another kamikaze and he died after inflicting only minor damage. But there were too many and now radical moves that spoiled aim for one enemy pilot only placed the destroyer in the path of another. Bombs and planes, bombs without planes and planes without bombs smashed against the defiant ship. A 20mm and 40mm mount amidships went up in flame, a bomb smashed into the after deckhouse and two kamikazes struck 5-inch mount number three, the lone 5-inch mount aft, killing six of the seven men within.

Holed, burning and with 71 of her living men bleeding, *Laffey* steamed on at high speed. What few guns that could operate continued to fire, damage control parties—seriously diminished by casualties—fought the several fires throughout the ship, and finally the battle was over. It ended because the 22 attacking planes had expended their ordnance, had been shot down (9 by *Laffey*) or had flown into the ship or ocean.

So badly damaged was *Laffey* from strafing, four bomb hits and six kamikaze crashes, that she had to be towed from the battle scene.

Temporary repairs and the lack of serious damage to the engineering spaces enabled her to steam for Saipan, thence to Eniwetok in the Marshall Islands and finally to Seattle, Washington, where she underwent repair from 24 May until 6 September 1945. Before workers began their healing work at Todd Shipyard, the navy opened the gates to the public so they might come and see the sacrifice of war. The aft 5-inch gun mount still showed the appalling 16 April destruction, as did other parts of the superstructure.

Standing near while the curious and the appreciative toured the damaged warship, some of those who remembered thinking they would have the story of Normandy to tell their children and grandchildren, now realized that story would be, at best, just a footnote to Okinawa, a battle still contested on that day. They thought, too, that this story would serve as a classic example of how control of the sea can lead to control of the land. But with a little more time, and time in which to read the faces of the civilians touring the scarred vessel, some concluded that this was not a story to tell any child or grandchild. It was a story that would inspire nightmares rather than an appreciation of valor.

In time, however, children become adults and the realities of life and death must be confronted. To this audience then, the veterans of *Laffey* have spoken. To this audience, valor and sacrifice are understood, and such an understanding leads some to allegiance to arms to defend their nation: for others such an understanding leads to work in the social and political arenas to ensure that such sacrifice and valor is not again required. Resting in her berth in Charleston Harbor, South Carolina, as part of the Patriots Point Naval and Maritime Museum, *Laffey* speaks to all who ask why she has been memorialized. But no matter what is said, or by whom, no words carry an eloquence equal to the actions of *Laffey's* crew on 16 April 1945 at a place called Okinawa.

USCGC INGHAM

ONE OF SEVEN 327 foot cutters of the "Secretary" class in honor of former Treasury Department Secretaries, USCGC *Ingham* WPG-35 (*Samuel L D. Ingham* until 1937) established one of the proudest, and longest, records of any ship to serve the United States. The keel of *Ingham* was laid at the Philadelphia Navy Yard on 1 May 1935, launch was 3 June 1936, and the cutter was commissioned 17 September 1936.

Three other units of the class were also built in Philadelphia: *Campbell* (WPG-32); *Duane* (WPG-33) and *Taney* (WPG-37). *Spencer* (WPG-36) and *Alexander Hamilton* (WPG-34) were built at the New York Navy Yard while *Bibb* (WPG-31) was built at the Charleston Navy Yard. *Ingham* also had a Charleston connection, undergoing APG conversion here during World War II (August-October 1944) among numerous port calls. All units of the class served with distinction during World War II and one, *Alexander Hamilton*, was lost 30 January 1942. All units are now gone except *Ingham* and *Taney*: *Taney* is preserved as a museum in Baltimore, Maryland.

Designed primarily for open ocean patrol and rescue, the 327 foot cutters displaced up to 2,750 tons, were capable of speeds up to 20 knots, could cruise approximately 9,500 miles at 11 knots on her two main engines, and carried a crew of 250 during World War II. Original main armament consisted of two 5 inch guns, but some units carried three during World War II. *Ingham* carried only two 5 inch guns during the 1941–45 war along with six 40 mm in twin mounts, four 20 mm and depth charges.

After commissioning, *Ingham* operated out of Port Angeles, Washington, until 1940 when she transferred to Boston. She saw service as a weather station in the Atlantic in 1940 before being stationed at Lisbon, Portugal, in early 1941. On 1 July 1941 *Ingham* was assigned to the Navy and spent 1942–43 in the North Atlantic, painted in wartime gray and blue camouflage colors. While operating as a convoy escort, she sank *U-*

USCGC Ingham *arrived at Patriots Point in 1989 after 52 years of distinguished service. On 15 December 1942* Ingham *sank U-626, and she received the Presidential Unit Citation for service off Vietnam.*

Many compartments aboard Ingham *have been preserved as they were at decommissioning in 1988. Manikins add a realistic effect.*

626 on 15 December 1942. Confirmed after the war, the sinking was not a "hole in one" attack, as legend has maintained, but instead was a well executed, by-the-book pattern.

Rescue duty in the North Atlantic included eight survivors of the SS *Tennessee* on 26 September 1942 and 33 survivors from the SS *Henry R. Mallory*, SS *West Portal* and SS *Robert E. Hopkins* on 7 February 1943. Additional survivors were picked up from the SS *Jeremiah Van Rensseler* and SS *Matthew Luckenbach* in the winter of 1943.

From the spring of 1943 into the summer of 1944 *Ingham* escorted convoys to the Mediterranean before transferring in late 1944 to the Pacific. As the U-boat problem in the Atlantic diminished, the remaining six members of the class were converted into Amphibious Force Flagships (AGC). In February 1945 *Ingham* served as flagship for the Mariveles-Corregidor (Philippines) Attack Group and the Tigbauan landings 18 March. On 29 March the cutter participated in the Negros Island landings and in July was flagship for the Balut Island Attack Unit. At the end of World War II, *Ingham* had

recorded 17 North Atlantic convoys, 12 Mediterranean convoys, two Caribbean convoys, six Pacific amphibious operations, and she saw occupation duty at Shanghai, Hong Kong, Indochina (Vietnam) and Formosa.

Returning to the Atlantic and her original white paint, *Ingham* was based at Norfolk, Virginia. Routinely, the high endurance cutter (WHEC) served in missions involving search and rescue, law enforcement, communications, research and weather. Not called to serve off Korea from 1950–53, the cutter was ordered to Vietnam in 1968. Called upon for gunfire support and surveillance, *Ingham* was also active in the blockade of the South Vietnam coast. For her 1968–69 Vietnam service, Operation Market Time in particular, *Ingham* was awarded the Presidential Unit Citation with Gold Star.

Returning to Portsmouth, Virginia, *Ingham* continued her peacetime routine, but with increased emphasis on the interception of drugs. In 1980, the cutter participated in the Mariel Boatlift from Cuba. After 52 years the cutter was decommissioned in May 1988 and transferred to Patriots Point. *Ingham* arrived in time for the

1989 Destroyer Escort Sailors Association (DESA) reunion, a fortunate occurrence in that many destroyer escorts were manned by Coast Guard personnel during World War II.

Ingham as a Museum

WHEN *Ingham* arrived at Patriots Point, a decision was made to present the cutter to the public as she was on her last day of active service. At the request of the *Ingham* veterans, the crews berthing compartment forward was cleared for an exhibit to tell the story of the cutter's history. That aside, the ship is as she was. Although there are no plans for her to return to operational status, she is the one vessel at Patriots Point that, with sufficient effort, could get underway again.

Among the more popular attractions to visitors (mostly along the starboard side compartments) on the main deck and second deck levels are several staterooms, the officer's pantry, CPO Mess, engine room, ship's office, crew's mess deck and officer's wardroom and mess. Aft, two heads (restrooms) are available for public use.

The former crew's mess converted to exhibit space now presents a large photographic history of the *Ingham* featuring construction and pre-war service, Atlantic, Mediterranean and Pacific combat during World War II, postwar assignments, and Vietnam combat. Memorabilia, models and uniforms enhance the exhibit as do artifacts from other vessels that encountered a similar history. In honor of Coast Guard personnel who served aboard destroyer escorts during World War II, the wheel, steering stand and other artifacts of the USS *Merrill* and other DEs are displayed.

Mounted on a starboard bulkhead where visitors board the cutter are several significant plaques. The smallest is *Ingham's* 1992 designation as a National Historic Landmark. A larger plaque honors the lone Coast Guard recipient of the Medal of Honor, Douglas Munro, who died in the line of duty at Guadalcanal in 1942. The largest series of plaques reflect *Ingham's* designation on 16 September 1996 by the Commandant of the Coast Guard as the "National Memorial to Coast Guardsmen killed in World War II and Vietnam." Over 40 separate ship plaques list the names of officers and men killed or missing in the two conflicts. Greatest losses during World War II included USCGC Escanaba WPG-77 (13 June 1943); USCGC *Muskeget* WAG-48 (9 September 1942); USS *Leopold* DE-319 (9 March 1944); and USS *Serpens* AK-94 (29 January 1945).

MARINE GROWTH ON CLAMAGORE AND YORKTOWN HULLS

WHILE VISITORS may notice that the submarine's sides are somewhat unsightly due to marine growth, it must be understood that she is sitting in a shallow water berth and is actually fully waterborne only about one hour before and after high tide. Since *Clamagore* sits on the bottom the majority of the time, the tide rises and falls up and down her hull resulting in a phenomenon, much like on *Yorktown*, where marine growth and corrosion are more prevalent and more visible in those areas of her sides where she is alternately exposed to both air and salt water.

It would be prohibitively expensive and potentially damaging to the thinner external skin encasing her trim tanks to frequently scrape and clean the barnacles and oysters from her sides. Also, the bottom on which she sits is not perfectly flat, resulting in her tendency to rest with a starboard list except at those times when she is fully waterborne. With her delicate trim and ballast systems, she often has a list until corrective action is taken, even when fully waterborne.

—DAVID BURNETT
Commander, USN, Ret.,
Patriots Point Engineer

USS Clamagore SS-343

Although the *Clamagore* (SS-343) was commissioned too late to see combat in World War II, and was later greatly modified from her original configuration, the submarine is still very popular with Patriots Point visitors. *Clamagore's* interior has not changed greatly over the years, and the submarine experience is easily captured while touring the boat (submarines are "boats" rather than "ships" in Navy terminology).

The Pacific war was won between 1941 and 1945 because U.S. Navy submarines closed the shipping lanes that were the economic lifelines of Japan. In addition to sinking enemy merchant and naval vessels, U.S. Navy submarines were utilized for numerous other functions. Before major amphibious landings, submarines were detailed to potential landing areas for reconnaissance. Aircraft would alert the enemy: submarines had a much better chance of remaining undetected. Further, submarines were used for rescue of downed pilots and transports for commando raids, scouting, mine laying, weather forecasting, picket boat destruction, and even shore bombardment against special targets such as refineries and railroads.

With only two percent of Navy personnel, the submarine force sank 55 percent of Japan's merchant ships. The submarines accounted for approximately 30 percent of Japanese warships, including several notable successes. One of the six Japanese carriers to strike Pearl Harbor, *Shokaku*, was sunk by *Cavalla* (SS-244) on 19 June 1944. That sinking has special meaning to Patriots Point as the museum's first executive director, Rear Admiral Herman J. Kossler, was the commanding officer of *Cavalla* on that day. Other Japanese carriers lost to U.S. Navy submarines included *Taiho*, sunk by *Albacore* (SS-219) in June 1944, and *Shinano* (originally intended to be Japan's third super-battleship) by *Archerfish* (SS-311). The only occasion a U.S. Navy submarine sank an enemy battleship was on 21 November 1944 when *Kongo* was sunk by *Sealion* (SS-195). In a final tabulation at the end of the war, *Flasher* (SS-249) recorded the greatest tonnage sunk and was the only submarine to account for more than 100,000 tons. *Tautog* (SS-199) sank the greatest number of enemy ships (26).

Of the 288 U.S. Navy submarines ready for duty in World War II, 52 were lost to all causes, 41 to enemy depth charges, air attack, surface gunfire, mines and shore batteries. Even with Japanese records available at the end of the war, there is still a question concerning the exact cause of nearly a quarter of the boats sunk. It is known that 38 boats were lost with all hands, and that 374 officers and 3,131 men are still on "eternal patrol." Viewed in terms of average personnel numbers assigned to the submarine force, these losses were very high.

Most World War II era submarines were named for

Heavily modified in 1947 and 1962, Clamagore shows little resemblance to her World War II appearance, but much of the interior is unchanged. USN

LEFT: *Like all submarines, the interior of* Clamagore *is cramped and there is optimum use of space.*

U. S. SUBMARINE CLAMAGORE
DOWN THE WAYS
FEBRUARY 25, 1945
ELECTRIC BOAT CO. GROTON, CONN.

USS Clamagore *(SS-343) was launched 25 February 1943 and commissioned 28 June 1945.*
Clamagore *did not see combat but served until decommissioned 27 June 1975.*   USN

fish. (Some more recent nuclear submarines are named for states, in part because of congressional funding campaigns and the knowledge by Navy officials that "fish don't vote.") *Clamagore* was a member of the highly successful 132 unit Balao class. Laid down 16 March 1944 at Electric Boat Company in Groton, Connecticut, the all-welded sub was launched 25 February 1945 and commissioned 28 June 1945 with Commander Sam C. Loomis, Jr., as her commanding officer. Originally nearly 312 feet long with a beam of 27 feet, the 1,526 ton boat mounted one 5-inch deck gun and two single 40mm anti-aircraft guns (forward and aft of the conning tower). Her main battery was ten torpedo tubes, six forward and four aft, for her two dozen 21-inch torpedoes. Her four 1,600 horsepower General Motors diesel engines provided a top speed of 20 knots on the surface. The crew was comprised of 8 officers and a crew of approximately 70 enlisted men.

Arriving in the Pacific just as the war ended, *Clamagore* operated in the Caribbean until 1947 when she was modernized into a Guppy II configuration. Fitted with a snorkel underwater air-intake system, she no longer had to surface to charge her batteries. Her sail was necessarily enlarged and deck guns were removed. After modernization, the boat continued training and operational missions in the Atlantic, Caribbean and Mediterranean. In late 1962 the submarine was again converted, this time to a Guppy III configuration, from which she emerged with a new 15 foot midsection which was required for new electronics. The bridge was completely enclosed within the sail, overall displacement rose to over 1,700 tons, and the boat had an increased range of 12,000 miles at 10 knots.

For most of her operational life, *Clamagore* was based at Key West, Florida, but after the Guppy III conversion in 1963, the boat transferred to New London, Connecticut. Scheduled for transfer to Turkey in the early 1970s, she was decommissioned after nearly 30 years of service on 27 June 1975. Mothballed at Philadelphia, the transfer to Turkey was cancelled and the boat was towed to Patriots Point in May 1981 and opened to the public in November.

Aboard the memorialized *Clamagore*, visitors immediately note the cramped space and the optimum use of the limited space. Only one compartment has been converted to exhibit space and that compartment is dedicated to the memory of the 52 submarines lost in World War II. Forty-seven individual submarine plaques list the names of officers and crew lost.

U.S. Navy Submarines Lost in World War II

Albacore	Growler	S-44
Amberjack	Grunion	Scamp
Argonaut	Gudgeon	Scorpion
Barbel	Harder	Sculpin
Bonefish	Herring	Sealion
Bullhead	Kete	Seawolf
Capelin	Lagarto	Shark SS-174
Cisco	Perch	Shark SS-314
Corvina	Pickerel	Snook
Darter	Pompano	Swordfish
Dorado	R-12	Tang
Escolar	Robalo	Trigger
Flier	Runner	Triton
Golet	S-26	Trout
Grampus	S-27	Tullibee
Grayback	S-28	Wahoo
Grayling	S-36	
Grenadier	S-39	

Battle Star Leaders

Narwhal SS-167 (15)
ThresherSS-200 (15)
Nautilus SS-168 (14)
Tautog SS-199 (14)
Plunger SS-179 (14)
Gato SS-212 (13)
Finback SS-230 (13)
Seawolf SS-197 (13)
Drum SS-228 (12)
Flying Fish SS-229 (12)
Silversides SS-236 (12)
StingraySS-186 (12)

Only one compartment within Clamagore *has been converted to exhibit space. That one compartment is dedicated to the 52 submarines lost in World War II.*

FROM 1975 when *Yorktown* entered Charleston Harbor as the first museum ship for the Patriots Point fleet, one major hurricane has struck and several others have barely missed. In 1996, two (Bertha and Fran) passed near Charleston before going ashore just north. Since 1989 the Charleston area has been fortunate to have been in the less damaging southern quadrant of several hurricanes.

Category four hurricane Hugo made a direct hit on Charleston 21–22 September 1989. Although well protected in Charleston Harbor, the ships of Patriots Point nonetheless suffered damage. *Yorktown* at high tide rests 20 feet in the mud. After Hugo, and today, the bow is still 20 feet but the stern is up to 25 feet. Utility fittings separated and three aircraft on the flight deck were damaged, the most serious being the loss of the canopy and starboard wing of a FJ Fury. *Laffey* and *Clamagore*, moored together starboard of the carrier, moved several feet and appeared to be making a torpedo run on Fort Sumter. *Ingham* was not damaged, but another long serving World War II Coast Guard Cutter, *Comanche*, was torn loose at the stern. *Comanche* swung around to port and pounded herself against the pier for two hours.

A local government helicopter lands aboard Yorktown *in July 1996 in anticipation of an aroaching hurricane. A crane assists in the removal of the submarine's brow. In the background is the framework of the present Charleston Harbor Hilton Hotel.*

Plans to repair her were not approved, and a few years later she was sunk off the coast of South Carolina as an artificial reef.

Active naval ships steam to the open sea to escape hurricanes or, if necessary, ride them out by always keeping their bow pointed into the storm. These options are not open to the ships of Patriots Point even though remaining at the pier leaves them vulnerable. This fact moves the Patriots Point staff to implementation of the museum's heavy weather plan when hurricanes present any potential threat to the South Carolina coast. Knowing the vagaries of hurricanes, the staff will begin preparation at least three days in advance of a storm. If probability of landfall near Mt. Pleasant increases, the staff will work around the clock to complete preparations with a goal of finishing all work 18 to 24 hours before the first storm bands arrive.

As preparation shifts into gear, a 20 ton crane is hired to move some aircraft from the flight deck to the hangar deck (if the strength of the storm warrants), and to remove brows between the pier and ships. On *Yorktown's* flight deck aircraft are double griped, helicopter blades are removed or folded, and straps are placed over cockpits. Without operational hydraulics to

HURRICANE PREPAREDNESS

After hurricane Hugo, 20-21 September 1989, a crane lifts a sunken boat from beside the Patriots Point pier. Note the displaced submarine and destroyer.

lock down wings, custom made battens are used to secure the exposed aircraft. Although planes on the hangar deck are well protected, they are griped anyway. All loose items such as benches and trash containers are moved and placed inside the hangar deck. After all local government helicopters are flown aboard and moved into the hangar deck, all hangar curtains and doors are closed.

The approach of a storm that could cause heavy damage will be from the east or northeast. Heavy easterly or northeasterly winds will force the *Clamagore* against the pier and put heavy pressure on the spring and bow lines of *Laffey* and *Ingham*. A tidal surge of 15 feet (surges at high tide are particularly dangerous) would place extreme stress on *Laffey* and *Ingham's* mooring lines, and could possibly break *Yorktown* free of the bottom. Responding to these threats, the staff will place additional mooring lines (up to 7 inches in diameter), close all doors and hatches, remove all shore power cables, unrig sewer, freshwater and phone lines, store all loose topside gear, and test all portable generators for emergency use. (During Hugo, anchors were dropped but with limited success). Ashore, display missiles are turned over and lashed together, and everything loose is secured. All aboard know preparations are nearing an end when ply-

wood is placed over the glass windows of the Ship's Store.

Within 12 hours of the storm's arrival, the museum is closed and most staff are dismissed to ensure their safety. The harbor is deserted as large ships have already left for the open sea. Waterfront buildings are secured with heavy equipment parked immediately in front of each closed door. In a large dockside parking lot usually filled with new cars to be shipped overseas, in July 1996 only an Army tank remained. Many pleasure boats not pulled from the water move up the Ashley, Cooper or Wando rivers as far as possible. White caps cover the harbor and ocean as far as the eye can see, while above, fast moving, low gray clouds allow diminishing views of blue sky and sunlight. Usual programming on radio and television is preempted for storm coverage and emergency instructions. High humidity is nearly always present during the summer months and therefore provides no indication of impending danger. About eight hours prior to landfall, the first dark outer band of the storm is overhead. Rain is intermittent and wind gusts are noticeable. With all flags down, the few remaining security staff aboard look to the windmill plane near the top of *Ingham's* mast for wind direction. Stress generated by hurricane preparation can be re-

HURRICANE PREPAREDNESS

lieved only when wind direction is from any direction other than east or northeast.

On the night of 21–22 September 1989, stress turned to excitement, exhilaration and fear as the storm, with all its noise of wind and heavy, horizontal rain, moved in. When the storm passed, the emotional state for many was pervasive depression. Extensive wind, water and tree damage to homes and businesses was compounded by a sudden "winter" landscape as nearly all leaves were blown from trees left standing. After a two-week period of clearing debris from roads and repairing basic utilities, hotels quickly filled with local residents forced from their homes along with an invasion of carpenters and roofers from throughout the southeast. In restaurants, the usual immediate seating turned into an hour or more wait as uprooted families and transient construction workers displaced usual customers at the tables. Normal time expended in grocery stores became protracted, and the familiar, normal everyday routine was interrupted at every turn. And, it continued, day after day, week after week.

Time began to heal wounds to the environment, to homes, businesses and finally emotions. A great contribution to the staff of Patriots Point and many others in the low country was the June 1990 appearance of Bob Hope aboard the *Yorktown* and his performance at The Citadel on behalf of the museum. Laughter lifted the spirits of all, depression dissipated, and anticipation of the future replaced memories of a most unhappy visit by Mother Nature. Within a full year after Hugo, most visible reminders of the storm in the Charleston area were gone. By 1991, it was all but forgotten. But today, and during every summer, there is no hesitancy at Patriots Point to err on the side of prudence in preparing for the next storm.

In World War II the USCGC Comanche *escorted convoys during the Battle of the Atlantic's darkest days. Donated to Patriots Point in 1983, the Cutter was damaged by Hurricane Hugo in September 1989. In October 1991 she was donated to the South Carolina Wildlife Department for use as a fishing reef.* Comanche *is seen here leaving her Patriots Point mooring for the last time.*

TBM-3 Avenger

B-25 Mitchell USAAF

4

Remembrance of Famous Carrier-based Aircraft and the Men Who Flew Them

Into 1998 over 30 fixed wing and rotary aircraft are in the Patriots Point Museum inventory. As a veteran of World War II, the *Yorktown* has on display all the combat aircraft that flew from her decks from 1943 through 1945 except for the very rare SB2C "Helldiver" dive bomber. Of all the major carrier-based aircraft to serve in World War II, all are now displayed aboard *Yorktown* except the SB2C and the Douglas TBD "Devastator." Arriving off Korea in late 1953, *Yorktown* was too late for combat operations, but the "Fighting Lady" did serve operationally off Vietnam. The two major carrier-based combat aircraft missing from the Patriots Point inventory that fought over Korea are the F9F Panther and the FH2 Banshee. Nearly all the major carrier combat aircraft that served during the Vietnam War are displayed either aboard *Yorktown* or land-side.

Even though responsible for the extensive restoration of several planes, very few on display belong to Patriots Point. Most were acquired through the National Museum of Naval Aviation at NAS Pensacola. A few were acquired from National Guard units or other museums. Patriots Point holds exclusive title only to the B-25 Mitchell and TBM-3 Avenger. All others are long term donations.

In the following descriptions of the aircraft displayed at Patriots Point, several qualifications need to be noted for listed statistics. Aircraft speed and range are affected by fuel and ordnance loads. Additional weight nearly always lowered speed and lessened range. Further, the amount of time a plane could stay airborne was effected by weight. The otherwise outstanding

F11F Tiger (removed from the museum in late 1998 after nearly 20 years on display) never adequately overcame her short time between launch and recovery aboard a carrier. And, over Vietnam, the fast A-4 Skyhawk became a relatively easy target for enemy planes and missiles when greatly slowed by heavy ordnance loads.

Although the machine-gun has not totally disappeared from fighter or attack aircraft since the end of World War II, it has become less a weapon of choice. Since the 1950s missiles have demonstrated greater use and reliability. The early heat-seeking air-to-air Sidewinder proved successful as well as the air-to-ground Bullpup missile. The radar beam over-the-horizon Phoenix missile has had no opportunity in combat, verification of hostile aircraft being the major impediment for its greater use.

Weight and size of an airplane is not as important as function. With the retirement of the World War II Essex class carriers through the 1970s, more modern carriers have been able to handle the heavier weight and landing speed of jets. Although range without in-flight refueling has remained similar between World War II aircraft and modern jets, conventional ordnance loads have dramatically increased. Further, technology has decreased the weight and size of nuclear weapons.

Few of the aircraft at Patriots Point are still flyable. In fact, the last thing the museum staff wants to see is one of its planes airborne (see "Hurricane" sidebar). However, several Patriots Point planes could be restored to flying status. Among these are the B-25, Sea Cobra, Sea King, TBM-3 Avenger, F-14 Tomcat and A-6 Intruder.

One of the few Grumman built Wildcats still in existence is Patriots Points' F4F-3A. The fighter is dedicated to Medal of Honor recipient Lt. Commander E.H. "Butch" O'Hare, the Navy's first World War II ace, and the man for whom the Chicago airport is named.

F4F-3A *Wildcat*

PULLED FROM Lake Michigan in 1988, the Wildcat displayed in Hangar Bay One aboard *Yorktown* was masterfully restored to mint condition by the Grumman Restoration Team in Bethpage, New York. Several members of the restoration team had built the original planes beginning in 1939. The Patriots Point Wildcat carries BuNo. 3956, one of only 95 F4F-3As manufactured.

Formally dedicated on 31 October 1993, the Patriots Point Wildcat honors the memory of Lt. Commander Edward Henry "Butch" O'Hare, USN. O'Hare was the U.S. Navy's first World War II ace and naval aviation's first WWII recipient of the Congressional Medal of Honor. On 20 February 1942 he flew alone into a flight of 8 Japanese bombers, destroying several and damaging others as he effectively broke-up the attack on his aircraft carrier, *Lexington* (CV-2). In November 1943 he was lost while successfully leading the first carrier night interception.

For the first 20 months of World War II, the Wildcat was the only carrier fighter to oppose the enemy in meaningful numbers. Lacking the speed, maneuverability and climb attributes of the Japanese Zero fighter, Wildcat pilots developed tactics to fully utilize their plane's rugged construction, diving speed and heavy armament of four .50 caliber machine guns in the F4F-3s and later FMs, and six guns in the F4F-4s. Research after World War II revealed the Wildcat recorded a 6.9-1 ratio over all enemy aircraft and it had a slight edge over the Zero.

Wartime production of the Wildcat was managed in the same manner as the TBF/TBM Avenger program. Grumman produced the F4F-3s (and F4F-3As), F4F-4s (folding wings, more armor protection, and four .50 guns) and experimental types while General Motors Eastern Aircraft Division produced nearly 4,500 FM-1s and FM-2s of the 6,037 total. Modified FMs proved to be especially suitable for U.S. Navy escort carriers while both Grumman and General Motors Wildcats found favor and utilization by the British. The fastest Wildcat was capable of speeds up to 332 mph: Maximum range was 900 miles (closer to 700 throughout 1942 and early 1943). The F4F-3A was powered by one 1,200 hp Pratt & Whitney R-1830-96. Later models had more powerful engines.

During World War II 107 F4F and FM Wildcat pilots died in combat or combat related operations while flying from 32 different aircraft carriers. *Enterprise* (CV-6) lost the most, 15.

F6F-5 Hellcat

F6F-5 Hellcat

EAGERLY AWAITED by U.S. Navy carrier fighter pilots, the successor to the F4F Wildcat proved to be well worth the wait. In all critical characteristics, the F6F Hellcat was a much more formidable opponent than the Wildcat, and it was easy fly. Top speed for the new Hellcat was 380 mph and maximum range was nearly 950 miles.

Grumman, original producer of the Wildcat, was the sole producer of the F6F Hellcat. Although built to compete against the Japanese Zero fighter, the first experimental Hellcat flew on 26 June 1942 shortly before the first Zero fell into Allied hands. By the end of World War II, Hellcats recorded a 19-1 victory ratio over enemy aircraft, nearly 75 per cent of U.S. Navy air to air victories. Standard armament consisted of six .50 guns with 400 rounds each. The F6F-5 model could also carry up to 2,000 pounds of bombs (or six rockets), which many did in the latter stages of the Pacific War. Power for the F6F-5 was supplied by one 2,000 hp Pratt & Whitney R-2800-10W engine.

Hellcat's were led into combat for the first time over Marcus Island on 31 August 1943 by CAG-5 (Air Group Five commanding officer) Commander James H. Flatley, Jr., flying from *Yorktown* (CV-10). The Patriots Point Hellcat (BuNo. 79593) is dedicated to Vice Admiral Flatley (1906–1958). Before the Marcus raid, Flatley had already earned the Navy Cross for air combat during the May 1942 Battle of the Coral Sea, and had led VF-10's "Grim Reapers" at the October 1942 Battle of Santa Cruz and the November 1942 Naval Battle of Guadalcanal.

Grumman produced nearly 12,300 Hellcats during World War II. Production ended in 1945, and the great World War II fighter saw limited use in the Korean War as an explosive guided missile drone.

Flying from 30 different carriers during World War II, 384 F6F Hellcat pilots made the supreme sacrifice while on combat missions. *Yorktown* (CV-10) topped the list with 45 killed in action.

FG-ID (F4U) Corsair

ONE OF THE MANY prized possessions on *Yorktown's* hangar deck is the inverted gull wing FG-ID (F4U) Corsair. Originally built by Chance Vought, the FG versions were built by Goodyear. Corsairs served the U.S. Navy from October 1942 into the middle 1950s. During World War II the Corsair had a 11:1 kill ratio and was the U.S. Navy's fastest fighter. As they did during World War II, Corsairs operated in fighter, night fighter

FG-1D (F4U) Corsair

lems did benefit the Marines who inherited the castoffs. Landing problems were solved by 1944 when the great speed of the Corsair was needed aboard carriers to serve as interceptors against kamikazes.

Funds for raising and restoring the Patriots Point FG-1D were donated by Charles Joseph McCarthy—who served as vice president of United Aircraft Corporation during the Corsair's design and development years, and by families, friends and 1939 Yale classmates in memory of Lt. Charles A. "Chuck" Pillsbury, USNR, who died in aerial combat on 2 November 1943 and Lt. Clement D. "Timmy" Gile, USNR. Both flew with VF-17, the first squadron to operate Corsairs from an aircraft carrier, *Bunker Hill* (CV-17).

Ninety-five Corsair pilots were killed in action off eleven different carriers during World War II, *Bennington* (CV-20) topping the list with 26. Another 95 were lost off 14 carriers during the Korean War, 23 from *Princeton* (CV-37).

and ground support roles during the Korean War.

The Corsair aboard *Yorktown* (BuNo. 88368), one of 12,200 produced in several variations and by three manufacturers, rested on the bottom of Lake Washington, Seattle, Washington, from 1947 until 1984 when it was raised and restoration work began. While the airframe was in relatively good condition, the original engine—currently in storage—was replaced within the plane during the restoration process. The engine used in the Patriots Point Corsair was one 2,000 hp Pratt & Whitney R-2800-8W.

Usual armament for the World War II F4U was six .50 machine guns and 2,000 pounds of bombs. Later models could carry up to 4,000 pounds of bombs or rockets and four 20mm cannon. Top speed was near 417 mph, ceiling was approximately 40,000 feet and range for World War II models was about 1,000 miles. Early in their careers, Corsairs were not used aboard carriers because of landing problems (poor vision over the long nose, too much bounce and structural deficiencies). The carrier suitability prob-

SBD-5 "Dauntless" Dive Bomber

Resting on *Yorktown's* hangar deck near the "Midway" exhibit since 1991 is one of the most famous and successful planes ever to fly from the deck of an aircraft carrier. The SBD "Dauntless" dive bomber is remembered as the plane that sank all four Japanese carriers at the June 1942 Battle of Midway. Flying from the decks of *Enterprise* (CV-6) and *Yorktown* (CV-5), SBDs sank Japanese carriers *Akagi, Kagi, Soryu* and *Hiryu*.

The Patriots Point SBD-5 is one of very few "true" Navy SBDs remaining in existence. Some SBDs seen in museum's are the U.S. Army version. The Patriots Point SBD-5 was restored by Mike Rettke after having been raised in 1987 from Lake Michigan after 44 years under water.

SBD DAUNTLESS

Dedication Speech, 2 October 1991

b y BARRETT TILLMAN

I AM GRATEFUL to Patriots Point for bringing me here to dedicate this splendid example of the Douglas SBD dive bomber. The combat record of the Dauntless and its war-winning effect in the Pacific five decades ago is well known to everyone present. But, I have access to insider knowledge that aircraft, like birds and other animals, lack any kind of institutional knowledge. When we're together with nobody else around, Dauntlesses tell me that they know only what they personally have experienced in their lifespan.

Therefore, I must ask the human participants to stand by for a few moments while I explain to SBD number 36173 something of its place in history.

Dauntless, you had 5,935 identical twins manufactured by Douglas Aircraft Company between the human years 1940 and 1944. The design genius named Edward H. Heinemann created you, with expert help from a variety of engineers and manufacturers at Northrop and Douglas. The first of your breed entered fleet service with the Marine Corps in 1940, filling a special requirement in naval aviation. Your mission is defined in your very designation: SBD, for Scout-Bomber by Douglas. You were produced in six models, including variants for the U.S. Army Air Forces. But you were made for the esoteric environment of the sea and the sky, which is the reason that tailhook is attached to your airframe. The U.S. Navy brought the art and science of dive bombing to near perfection, for no other means of attack so suited the requirement of putting ordnance on a fast ship maneuvering in open water.

But your first day at war wasn't very successful, Dauntless. Two squadrons from the carrier *Enterprise* were caught over Pearl Harbor on 7 December 1941, and several of them were shot down by Japanese carrier planes. From there your kind began its painful way toward Tokyo. There were faltering first steps with hit and run carrier raids on

SBD DAUNTLESS

enemy bases across the central Pacific. But along the way your aircrews and those who fueled, armed and serviced you grew in strength and knowledge and confidence. Your kind were instrumental in sinking enemy carriers during the turbulent six months of 1942: at Coral Sea, wonderfully well at Midway, and throughout the long travail at a mysterious place called Guadalcanal. In that period you sank more enemy warships than the rest of the U.S. Navy combined, and became the worst enemy of Imperial Japan.

But I want you to know, Dauntless, that your twins were not limited to action in the Pacific. They were found aboard carriers wherever the U.S. Navy sailed, including theaters as far flung as North African waters and the frigid arena off Norway. In short, wherever carrier air power was needed, your kind were there.

The apogee of your career came two years after Midway, off the Marianas in June 1944. By then your kind had largely been replaced by supposedly better dive bombers, the kind built by Curtiss. But when Bombing 10 and 16 returned from that mission beyond darkness, there were only three SBDs missing, compared to 45 of the 50 Helldivers. The following month you left front-line carrier service, but soldiered on with the Marines in the central Pacific and the Philippines.

Now I realize, Dauntless, that all this must have seemed far away and strange to you, considering that you were produced in 1944 and mainly served in Training Command. And when that ham-fisted young ensign trying to qualify on the Great Lakes put you into the water, you surely must have thought that you had slipped from the world of men and the sky forever. You were on the bottom of Lake Michigan 44 years before men cared enough to seek you out and raise you back into the clear air, then lovingly, skillfully, restore you to like-new condition.

And what a revelation that must have been for you! I try to imagine how you felt the first time you heard a vacuum-cleaner whine in the air and saw incredibly fast flying machines that somehow fly without propellers. Well, that's a longer story, Dauntless, and I won't dwell on it here.

But I do want you to know a couple of things that I feel so deeply. As you sit here today, your tires firmly planted on a carrier deck once more, you will find the same kind of loving attention that you knew in your youth. In short, I want to say welcome back, Dauntless. Welcome back to the world of ships and men.

But more than that, Dauntless. I want to say "Welcome home."

Fund raising for the restoration was shared by Patriots Point, the Yorktown Association and the family of Ensign Samuel J. Underhill, USNR, a pilot killed during the May 1942 Battle of the Coral Sea while flying an SBD in defense of his ship, the first carrier *Yorktown* (CV-5).

SBDs entered service in 1940 and served through the end of World War II in 1945. One of 5,935 produced by Douglas Aircraft Company between 1940 and 1944, the Patriots Point SBD carries BuNo. 36173. Used for scouting and training as well as dive bombing, the SBD was designed by Edward H. Heinemann. Top speed was 245 mph and maximum range was 1,100 miles for the single engine 1,200 hp Wright R-1820-60 SBD-5. The well-liked, dependable plane normally carried a bomb load of 500 to 1,000 pounds but was designed to carry up to 1,900. The Dauntless served aboard *Yorktown* (CV-10) in 1943 and 1944 before being replaced by the SB2C "Helldiver."

During World War II, 115 "Dauntless" pilots were killed in action. Fifty-six were lost off *Enterprise* (CV-6).

TBM-3E Avenger

AMONG THE FIRST aircraft to be displayed aboard *Yorktown* (1976) was a TBM-3E Avenger. On 4 June 1942, six TBF Avengers flew into the Battle of Midway, the first occasion the torpedo-bomber was used operationally. Five were lost on that mission, but by the end of World War II, the Avenger proved to be highly successful. Avengers delivered fatal torpedo blows to both Japanese super-battleships (*Yamato* and *Musashi*) and the IJN aircraft carrier *Hiyo* in addition to many other enemy ships. With a 2,000 pound internal bomb-bay capacity, the TBF/TBM was an effective bomber against land installations and submarines.

Developed by the Bethpage, New York, Grumman Aircraft Corporation(TBF designation), wartime expansion required another manufacturer, General Motors, Eastern Aircraft Division (TBM) headquartered in Trenton, New Jersey. Grumman and General Motors produced a total of 9,836 Avengers with some planes serving operationally into 1954. Originally accommodating a pilot, radar operator and gunner, Avengers were capable of a top speed near 270 mph and had a range of approximately 1,200 miles. Some versions had up to two forward-firing .50 machine guns while most carried one dorsal .50 caliber and one ventral .30 caliber machine gun. A large airplane (about 10,500 pounds empty and nearly 18,000 fully loaded) and heavy on the controls, it was nonetheless an excellent ordnance platform. The engine for the TBM-3E was one 1,900 hp Wright R-2600-20.

The TBM-3E Avenger aboard *Yorktown* is dedicated to the memory of VT-5 skipper Lt. Commander Richard Upson, who was killed in action over Truk, 30 April 1944. Perhaps the best known Avenger pilot is former president George Bush. Then Lt.j.g. Bush was shot down over Chichi Jima on 2 September 1944 while flying from *San Jacinto* (CVL-30). His plane was painted in the same tri-color scheme as the Avenger aboard *Yorktown*.

B-25D Mitchell

ALTHOUGH THE B-25 aboard *Yorktown* may seem to be out of place, there was a World War II connection between the Army Air Force medium bomber and the U.S. Navy. First available to the Army Air Corps in 1939 and named in honor of Brigadier General Billy Mitchell, 676 B-25s were used by the Navy (designated "PBJ Mitchell") beginning in early 1943. Navy versions of the fast, maneuverable bomber usually carried radar and depth charges in addition to bombs for anti-submarine warfare.

The most memorable connection between the B-25 and the U.S. Navy was the Halsey-Doolittle Raid. On 18 April 1942, sixteen B-25Bs lifted from the deck of the aircraft carrier *Hornet* (CV-8) to attack Tokyo and other Japanese cities. Damage was minimal, but it did provide an early-war emotional lift for American morale in addition to impacting enemy strategy. A pictorial story of the famous raid is presented with mementos on a portside bulkhead near the suspended B-25 on *Yorktown's* aft hangar deck.

The Patriots Point plane (arrived 1981) is a B-25D-NC Mitchell II (AC # 41-29784) built by North American Aviation at Kansas City rather than the main base at Inglewood, California. This model was capable of 295 mph with her two 1,700 Wright Cyclone R-2600 engines, had a normal range of 2,000 miles and a crew of five. Bomb load ranged from 2,400 to 3,200 pounds and the D carried five machine-guns (some other models carried up to 15 machine-guns and some C and G versions carried a tank-buster .75 cannon). By the end of World War II approximately 10,000 B-25s had been manufactured with many being transferred to allied forces.

After the war, a large number of B-25s were converted for civilian use to recoup wartime costs and to meet civilian market demand for a fast, dependable corporate aircraft. The Patriots Point B-25 was used by the E.I. Dupont Corporation which donated the plane soon after the establishment of the museum.

Stearman N2S Kaydet

ONE OF MANY PLANES on long term loan to Patriots Point from the National Museum of Naval Aviation, NAS Pensacola, is a Stearman N2S Kaydet, the only biplane aboard *Yorktown*. A plane familiar to any World War II era U.S. Navy pilot, the Stearman was used as a trainer beginning in 1935 in both land and float plane versions. Serving the Navy and the Army Air Force, over 8,000 were manufactured by the Stearman Aircraft Division (a subsidiary of Boeing Aircraft Company) located in Wichita, Kansas.

The Stearman looked very much like the N3N primary trainer built by the Naval Aircraft Factory at Philadelphia, Pennsylvania. The N3N was first termed "The Yellow Peril" by student pilots and instructors because of its predominantly yellow paint and relatively inexperienced pilots, but the Stearmans also shared the sobriquet.

In service with the Air Force until 1948 and the Navy until 1961, the Kaydet had a top speed of only 125mph, a ceiling over 11,000 feet and a range of approximately 500 miles. The engine for the Patriots Point Stearman was the Lycoming R-680-8. The student occupied the rear seat for solo flights. Following completion of primary flight training during the World War II era, a student pilot in training with the Navy advanced to the North American SNJ Texan (and the front seat) for instrument and cross country training before moving on to operational aircraft. Between 1987 and 1994 an SNJ was on display at Patriots Point, but was returned to the National Museum of Naval Aviation.

Stearman N2S Kaydet

AD-4N Skyraider

AD-4N Skyraider

THE PATRIOTS POINT AD-4N Skyraider, a Korean War carrier-based attack aircraft, was beautifully restored in 1992 and acquired by the museum in 1993. During the Cold War era, the Skyraider was one of the Navy's first planes capable of carrying a scaled-down tactical nuclear weapon.

Originally designed as a single-seat, dive bomber/torpedo plane, the highly successful design resulted in a total production of 3,180, and was continually modified and improved through-

F-8K Crusader

out its 12 year production period (1945–1957). Manufactured by the Douglas Aircraft Company at El Segundo, California, the Skyraider had a gross weight over 18,000 pounds, was powered by one 2,700 hp Wright R-3350-26W, had a top speed of nearly 320 mph, a service ceiling close to 32,000 feet and a range of approximately 900 miles.

One of the best close support aircraft of all time, the "Flying Dump-truck" usually carried two to four 20mm cannon and up to 8,000 pounds of bombs, rockets, depth charges, mines or a torpedo, all externally. Skyraiders were also utilized in night operations and for reconnaissance, countermeasures and transport.

The Patriots Point AD-4N Skyraider (BuNo. 127007) is dedicated to both Lt. Commander Harold "Swede" Carlson, USN(Ret), and to Rear Admiral Arthur K. Knoizen, USN(Ret). Carlson led the bombing attacks on North Korean bridges, identified in 1951 as "Carlson's Canyon." Several months later, he was cited for leading the aerial torpedo attacks that destroyed the Hwachon Dam in North Korea, thus saving the lives of thousands of Marine and Army ground troops. Knoizen flew more than 100 Skyraider combat missions in both Korea and Vietnam. Eighty of those were as commanding officer of VA-165 aboard the *Coral Sea* (CVA-43) in the Tonkin Gulf during the late 1960's. Later, he

served as executive assistant to the Chairman of the Joint Chiefs of Staff.

Flying from 11 different carriers during the Korean War, 44 pilots were killed in action. Over Vietnam, another 32 were lost from 10 different carriers.

F-8K Crusader

During the Cold War, probably no other fighter attracted more attention in the Soviet Union than the F-8 Crusader. Operational aboard carriers from 1957, the supersonic Crusader could achieve air superiority immediately upon arriving in an area of crisis or conflict. Before leaving front-line service, the Crusader earned the sobriquet "MiG Master."

Developed by Chance Vought before being absorbed into Dallas, Texas, based Ling-Temco-Vought (LTV), over 1,200 Crusaders were manufactured between 1956 and the early 1960s. The Patriots Point Crusader, BuNo. 146939, was originally an F-8C but received the "K" designation after being remanufactured in 1967. Powered by one Pratt & Whitney J57-P-16 turbojet, the Crusader was capable of speeds near 1,100 mph and a range of 1,100 miles. Standard armament consisted of four 20mm cannon, two to four Sidewinder missiles, and as much as

5,000 pounds of ordnance. All ordnance except the cannon were carried externally.

The Patriots Point Crusader is dedicated to two Navy pilots. The portside honors Capt. Robert W. "Duke" Windsor, who as a commander did carrier suitability and evaluation testing of the F-8 (1955–57), and was awarded the Thompson Speed Trophy for first breaking the 1,000 mph speed barrier while flying a Crusader in August 1956. The starboard side is dedicated to Rear Admiral Robert H. Shumaker, the second aviator shot down and captured in Vietnam 11 February 1965. One of the "Alcatraz Gang," he was released 12 February 1973.

Active over Vietnam, 15 Crusader pilots were lost from six carriers. Three each were lost from *Bon Homme Richard* (CV-31), *Oriskany* (CV-34) and *Midway* (CV-41).

A-4L Skyhawk

On display aboard *Yorktown* since 1989 is a A-4L Skyhawk, often referred to as "Heinemann's Hot Rod." Ed Heinemann designed the plane for Douglas in the early 1950s as a close support attack aircraft. A successful attack jet during the Vietnam War, the Skyhawk was also used for many years by the Blue Angels. In an accompanying picture, the A-4L is shown being lifted aboard *Yorktown* upon her arrival.

Currently on display on *Yorktown's* flight deck, the Skyhawk carried only a pilot, and was renowned for its ability to carry up to 9,155 pounds of ordnance—plus two 20mm guns—with its own empty weight being just 10,465 pounds. Powered by one Pratt and Whitney turbojet since 1961, Skyhawks could reach a top speed of 670 miles per hour. The Patriots Point

A-4L Skyhawk

Skyhawk, BuNo. 149623, was an early version (circa 1959) powered by one Wright J-65-W-20. Like many Marine Corps and Navy carrier based aircraft, range was modest; less than 350 miles with a medium bomb load. Retired from front-line service with U.S. armed forces after more than 30 years of service beginning in 1954, some of the nearly 3,000 Skyhawks are still used by several countries.

The Patriots Point Skyhawk is dedicated to Congressional Medal of Honor recipient Vice Admiral James B. Stockdale who was shot down over Vietnam in 1965. The senior naval officer among the prisoners of war in Hanoi for seven and a half years, he was unbroken by continuous torture during interrogation and refused to be used for propaganda purposes. His example of character and leadership serves as a model for all confronted by adversity.

Like many of the aircraft at Patriots Point, the Skyhawk rests beside a memorial plaque. The Skyhawk plaque honors 73 pilots lost in combat over Vietnam from 14 different carriers. Fourteen pilots were lost from *Oriskany* (CV-34). Light enough to serve on modernized Essex class carriers, Skyhawks were lost over Vietnam from five Essex class carriers that won battle stars in the Pacific during World War II.

F-4J Phantom II

INHERITING THE NAME of the U.S. Navy's first Phantom (FD/FH), the McDonnell-Douglas F-4 Phantom II was a very successful aircraft. The large, fast plane was used by the Navy, Air Force and Marines, serving in operational status from 1960 through the Persian Gulf War in 1991. Originally intended to be a high altitude interceptor, its major utilization over Vietnam was for long range strikes. Still, the F-4 Phantom II accounted for over half the North Vietnamese aircraft shot down during the war. In the Persian Gulf War, its major function ("Wild Weasel") was to destroy Iraqi radar installations.

The Patriots Point F-4J Phantom II, BuNo. 153077, was powered by two J79-GE-10 turbojets and could reach a speed of nearly 1,500 mph. The Phantom II is a very large plane compared to earlier fighter interceptor designs. The F-4 has a maximum weight of over 54,000 pounds compared to 42,000 for the F-8 Crusader and 22,000 for the F11F-1 "Tiger." Like other jets of its era, the Phantom could fly across the United States without refueling, but the two-man (in tandem) aircraft had only a 900 mile range for combat operations. Air to air armament consisted entirely of missiles. For strike missions the Phantom II could carry up to 16,000 pounds of ordnance.

The Patriots Point F-4J Phantom II, currently painted on the starboard side in the colors of VF-31 during deployment aboard *Saratoga* (CV-60), is dedicated to Rear Admiral James H. Flatley III and his VF-31 radar officer, Lt. Commander Bud Dougherty. Flatley flew 344 combat missions over Vietnam during three deployments, receiving a Silver Star and two Distinguished Flying Crosses. At retirement in 1987, Flatley held the record for 1,607 carrier landings. The eldest son of the famous World War II fighter pilot, Vice Admiral James H. Flatley, Jr., Rear Admiral Flatley currently is Chief Executive Officer for Patriots Point. Portside markings honor the Marine Corps team of Major Lee Lassiter and Captain John Cummings who shot down a MIG over Vietnam in 1972.

Thirty-five F-4 Phantom pilots and RIOs were lost over Vietnam from seven different carriers. Ten were lost from *Kitty Hawk* (CV-63).

A-7E Corsair II

SOON AFTER THE LAST of Ling-Temco-Vought's successful F-8 Crusader was manufactured, the LTV Aerospace Corporation began production of an equally successful carrier-based light attack plane to succeed the A-4 Skyhawk. Although similar in appearance to the Crusader, the function, and therefore the development, of the A-7 Corsair II was different.

In late 1967 the A-7 made its first strike and close support flights in combat over Viet-

F-4J Phantom

A-7E Corsair II

nam. Although not used as a fighter throughout its 24 year service life, the A-7 Corsair II was equal to the success of the earlier, piston-powered F4U Corsair.

The Patriots Point A-7E Corsair II (arrived 1994) served over Vietnam and saw combat service in the 1991 Persian Gulf War. The single seat A-7E was powered by one Allison TF-41-A-2 turbofan, had a top speed of nearly 700 mph and a combat range of approximately 700 miles (ferry range was about 3,000 miles). Armament consisted of one 20mm multi-barrel gun and up to

Admiral George E.R. "Gus" Kinnear, USN, Ret., (middle) stands beside the A-7E dedicated to him.

15,000 pounds of ordnance, about four to five times the ordnance capacity of the F4U Corsair.

The Patriots Point A-7E is dedicated to two outstanding pilots. The portside, painted in appropriate colors, honors Admiral George E.R. "Gus" Kinnear II, who as a Commander in 1967 led the first major A-7s (VA-147) AIR WING strikes over Hanoi from *Ranger* (CV-61). The starboard side is dedicated to Commander Mark Fitzgerald of VA-46. The starboard side is painted in the colors displayed on the plane while in service aboard the *John F. Kennedy* (CV-67), and shows the aircraft's original BuNo. 159291.

Twenty-one pilots were lost over Vietnam from seven different carriers. Five were lost from *America* (CV-66).

A-6E Intruder

FEW CARRIER-BASED AIRCRAFT ever possessed a name that better described its function more appropriately than the A-6E Intruder. The versatile, heavily armed A-6 found its targets in Vietnam and the Middle East from high and low altitude both day and night and in all weather conditions. Operational from 1962 into 1997, the Grumman-built Intruder has been so successful that subsequent aircraft will be hard pressed to match its record.

Particularly adept at attacking targets by flying below radar detection, the Intruder carries a pilot and weapons officer side-by-side in the cockpit. Powered by two Pratt & Whitney J52-P-8 turbojets, the Intruder has a top speed of approximately 650 mph, a combat range of nearly 1,100 miles, and is capable of carrying 17,000 pounds of ordnance. Primarily a strike bomber, some variants of the Intruder have been used for electronic countermeasures and even as a tanker.

The Patriots Point A-6E Intruder, BuNo. 152599, is dedicated to six naval aviators. The

A-6E Intruder

portside is dedicated to Rear Admiral Jeremiah A. Denton and his weapons officer, then Lt.j.g. Bill Tschudy. Shot down 18 July 1965 flying from *Independence* (CV-62), Commander Denton was one of the "Alcatraz Gang" before being repatriated 12 February 1973. Recipient of the Navy Cross among other decorations, following retirement he was elected to the United States Senate from Alabama. Honored on the starboard side of the A-6E are Lt. Commander Barry Cooke and Lt. Patrick Connor, both of VA-36 lost from *Theodore Roosevelt* (CVN-71) during the Persian Gulf War, and Lt. Mark Lange and Lt. Bobby Goodman of VA-85 aboard *John F. Kennedy* (CV-67) during the raid on Lebanon 4 December 1983. Lt. Lange did not survive that mission.

Over Vietnam, 58 aviators were lost from nine different carriers, 17 having been lost from *Kitty Hawk* (CV-63). Over Lebanon in 1983 and during the Persian Gulf War, another five were lost including the two listed above from CVN-71 and two from the *Ranger* (CV-61).

F-14A Tomcat

PROMINENTLY FEATURED in the movie "Top Gun,' the F-14A Tomcat (BuNo. 159025) is particularly popular with visitors to Patriots Point. Developed too late for service over Vietnam (first deliveries to squadrons began in late 1972), the Mach 2 plus, "swing-wing" Grumman-built fighter did

F-14A Tomcat

S-2E Tracker

see action during the Persian Gulf War. A proven air superiority fighter, the Tomcat is still in operational status (1999) and is scheduled to remain in service until early in the 21st century.

Crewed by a pilot and naval flight officer seated in tandem, the plane is capable of speeds near 1,500 mph. Original engines for the F-14A were two Pratt & Whitney TF30-P-412 turbofans which, although improved over time, proved to be a problem for the aircraft throughout much of its service life. Capable of carrying a wide array of air-to-air and air-to-ground weapons, the Tomcat's electronic systems can track 24 targets at great distances and engage six simultaneously. Total armament capacity is approximately 14,500 pounds, including the M61 20mm cannon located on the portside of the aircraft near the cockpit. A heavy plane (up to 72,000 pounds at take-off), the F-14A can remain in the air up to four hours with an internal fuel capacity near 2,400 gallons and longer if refueled in-flight. Of course, combat operations greatly reduce range.

While the Tomcat is first and foremost an air superiority interceptor, it can be utilized for attack and multi-sensor reconnaissance. No longer in production, the Tomcat is being supplanted by the F-18 Hornet.

S-2E Tracker

Soon after the Cold War began, Soviet submarines armed with missiles posed a new threat to the United States. One early anti-submarine practice of the U.S. Navy centered on using some aircraft with radar to track Soviet submarines and other planes to attack. In the early 1950s, Grumman Aircraft Corporation developed the Tracker which could both track and attack submarines.

Operating from aircraft carriers and land bases from 1954 into the 1970s, the S-2 Tracker was capable of speeds from 250 to 285 mph. However, stability at slow speed was a more important consideration. The relatively small S-2 (less than 27,000 pounds gross) was powered by two 1,525 hp Wright R-1820-82WAs, could lift off a carrier without a catapult, and had a normal range of approximately 1,200 miles.

The basic function of the plane required two pilots and two radar operators. To find an enemy submarine, the Tracker was equipped with a retractable search radar (bottom), a retractable magnetic anomaly detector, or "MAD" (rear), a 70 million candlepower searchlight (starboard wing), and sono-buoys (rear of engine

E-1B Tracer

both aerial and surface targets to distances over 200 miles. Further, the E-1B radar could be used to direct friendly aircraft to a hostile target regardless of weather conditions and darkness.

Originally the E-1B was designated WF-2, which led crewmembers to assign the nickname "Willy Fudd" to the plane. Although newer planes carrying more sophisticated radar have made the Tracer obsolete, the availability of the E-1B in 1958 was a major advancement not only in surveillance but also in aerial and surface strategy and tactics.

Powered by the same engines as the S-2 Tracker, the Patriots Point E-1B, BuNo. 147225, served on seven different carriers from 1961 through 1975. When retired it had over nine months of flying time. Tracers and Trackers served aboard *Yorktown* the last decade of the carrier's operational life, and they were among the very first planes to arrive aboard after the carrier was transferred to museum status.

nacelles). For attack, the Tracker could carry up to 4,800 pounds of ordnance including bombs, rockets, depth charges and sonar/acoustic homing torpedoes in an internal weapons bay and under the wings.

The Patriots Point S-2E Tracker, BuNo. 151657, is dedicated to the memory of Commander Donald R. Hubbs, CO of VS-23, and his aircrew, Lt. j.g. Lee D. Benson, AX2 Randall Nightingale and ADRAN Thomas D. Barber who were lost off Vietnam on 17 March 1968 operating from *Yorktown* (CV-10). During the Vietnam War 12 aviators were lost in Trackers from three different carriers (four each from *Yorktown*, *Hornet* CV-12 and *Kearsarge* CV-33).

E-1B Tracer

BUILT BY THE SAME CORPORATION (Grumman) that built the S-2 Tracker, the E-1B Tracer was essentially a slightly wider Tracker with a modified tail configuration. Other than the triple tail, the most obvious difference between the two aircraft was the very large oval radome atop the E-1B. The powerful airborne radar assured surveillance for

UH-34D Seahorse

THE UH-34D SEAHORSE (originally designated HUS-1) played a significant role during *Yorktown's* operational service as an anti-submarine carrier (CVS). Relative to most other aircraft displayed on *Yorktown's* flight deck, the Seahorse appears benign.

However, the major function of the Seahorse made it as lethal as many of the other aircraft displayed aboard CV-10.

Entering active service in 1955, the Seahorse operated as a hunter of foreign submarines and it had the potential to be a killer. Using radar and dipping sonar (ASDIC) for underwater search, a Seahorse could launch sonar/acoustic homing torpedoes at an underwater target. Normal procedure was to launch torpedoes from an altitude of

*UH-34D
Seahorse*

approximately 60 feet with the Seahorse either hovering or moving at speeds up to 100 mph.

Manufactured by Sikorsky Aircraft Division of United Aircraft Corporation in Stratford, Connecticut, the single engine (1,525 hp Wright R-1820-84) Seahorse was capable of nearly 120 mph. It carried two pilots and up to 18 passengers. Hampered by short range, less than 300 miles, the Seahorse was widely used both by the Navy and Marines in the additional roles of transport, search and rescue.

The Patriots Point Seahorse, BuNo. 147171, was primarily utilized by the Marines and came aboard *Yorktown* for display in 1975.

H-3 Sea King

LARGER (19,000 to 14,000 pounds gross) and faster (165 to 123 mph) than the earlier UH-34 Seahorse, the Sikorsky-built, two-engine (T58-GE-10) H-3 Sea King was intended to be an improved anti-submarine helicopter. Whereas the earlier short-range Seahorse operated in pairs, one to find the target and the second to attack, the newer H-3 Sea King was designed to fulfill both roles. The Sea King with four-man crews, two pilots and two radar operators, had a range over 600 miles, which was nearly double the capabil-

H-3 Sea King

Capt. Robert S. Vermilya, USN, Ret., decorated Vietnam War Sea King pilot. USN

ity of the Seahorse. Too, the practice of refueling from FRAM modified destroyers enabled the Sea King to remain airborne for even longer missions. The watertight hull and stabilizing floats, which also housed retractable wheels, provided amphibious capability.

While successful in the primary all-weather, anti-submarine role for which it was designed, the Sea King was equally successful as a search and rescue (SAR) helicopter. Operational in 1961 before the beginning of major American involvement in the Vietnam War, Sea King's rescued many downed aviators. Numerous rescues were made while under fire, and a number of Sea King's were lost while attempting rescues. Machine-guns were installed on SAR helicopters for defensive purposes.

The Patriots Point Sea King is dedicated in honor of Captain Robert S. Vermilya, USN(Ret), who was awarded the Silver Star and Bronze Star for heroism during rescue missions in Vietnam. Nine carrier-based aviators from two carriers (*Hornet* CV-12 and *Constellation* CV-64) were lost during the Vietnam War. Other losses occurred from land-based squadrons.

Sea King, BuNo. 149932, was flown aboard *Yorktown* in January 1994, and is the only plane to have flown aboard *Yorktown* for display. However, several other planes displayed at Patriots Point did fly into the Charleston area before being transported to the ship to be lifted aboard by a crane.

UH-1 Helicopters

ALL THE AIRCRAFT at Patriots Point represent military history. Except for the A-7 Corsair on *Yorktown's* flight deck, only the two UH-1 helicopters displayed land-side in the Advanced Tactical Support Base experienced combat. One, U.S. Army serial number 66-15005, a UH-1C reconfigured to a UH-1M "Mike" gunship in

UH-1

1971, was seriously damaged by gunfire in Vietnam seven times with one killed and one wounded. The "Mike" was acquired by the Army in January 1967 and served through 1972 before being transferred to the Army National Guard. As a UH-1M, the "Mike" was armed with two M-21 six-barrel miniguns, two rocket launchers (seven-tube 2.75 inch rockets) and various caliber machine-guns operated by door gunners. Navy units played a significant role in controlling inland waterways in Vietnam. "Game Wardens" used the helicopter gunships to both cover and support patrol boats, river and coastal operations plus river transportation throughout the Mekong Delta. Thus, the Navy markings on 66-15005. The Patriots Point UH-1M served with the New Jersey Army National Guard through 1991 and was transported to Mt. Pleasant in 1993.

The second UH-1 helicopter, serial number 65-10132, was configured as a UH-1H for rapid medical evacuation. Damaged once in Vietnam, it was acquired by the U.S. Army in August 1966 and served through December 1975. It was transferred to Patriots Point from the U.S. Army Aviation Museum, Fort Rucker, Alabama, in 1993.

Both UH-1's ("Hueys") were manufactured by Bell Helicopter Company, Fort Worth, Texas. The UH-1 could function as utility transports (up to 14 passengers), trainers and reconnaissance aircraft as well as assault and rescue air-

AH-1J Sea Cobra

craft. Powered by one Lycoming T53-L engine, the UH-1 could fly at 125 mph with a range just under 300 miles. Maximum take-off weight was nearly 10,000 pounds (6,000 empty).

AH-1J Sea Cobra

WHEREAS THE HU-1 helicopters were configured to fulfill several roles, the Bell AH-1 Sea Cobra is designed only for combat operations. Developed during the Vietnam War, the Sea Cobra demonstrated its deadly capability against tanks, fortifications and personnel during the Persian Gulf War. Used by the U.S. Army and the Marine Corps, the AH-1J is powered by a Pratt & Whitney T400-CP-400 Twin Pac, can reach speeds of nearly 130 mph and has a range of approximately 300 miles. A few AH-1Js were manufactured as an improved AH-1T demonstrating improved performance and ordnance capability.

The Patriots Point Sea Cobra, BuNo. 159210, is armed with a XM-197 three-barrel 20mm in the nose tactical turret. On the stub wings, the AH-1J can carry a wide range of ordnance including gun pods, rockets or grenade launchers. The narrow configuration of the Sea Cobra limits the crew to a gunner and pilot seated in tandem. Transferred to Patriots Point in 1993, the USMC Sea Cobra was flown to its present site from NAS Atlanta.

Gyrodyne Drone Helicopters

TWO LIGHT DRONE HELICOPTERS are on display at Patriots Point. Developed by the Long Island, New York based Gyrodyne Company between 1958 and 1960, the program continued production into 1970. The basic function of the drone was to perform anti-submarine operations from the decks of World War II era destroyers, primarily Sumner and Gearing class destroyers. The weapon system's first letters of "drone anti-submarine helicopter" provided the common sobriquet "DASH" for the aircraft. Although the system proved successful, sailors, as always, found

QH-50A

another nickname for the DASH; "down at sea helicopter."

Currently suspended in Hangar Bay III is the QH-50A, one of nine original developmental models. One early claim to fame was the grand prize for the most maneuverable helicopter at the 1961 Paris Air Show. Equipped with a 72 hp Porsche reciprocating engine, the developmental "A" models often carried a pilot. Production models, however, were unmanned.

Located aboard *Laffey* is a QH-50C production model, a type that once operated from *Laffey* and other destroyers during the 1960s and early 1970s. The modernized Sumner and Gearing class destroyers were fitted with a hangar for two drones and a landing platform. Audio command signals controlled the drones near the ship and were guided by radar when over the horizon. Weighing nearly 1,200 pounds empty with a capability to carry another 1,000 pounds of ordnance and fuel, and powered by a 300 shp Boeing gas turbine engine, the "C" could fly nearly 100 mph, had a combat radius of 30 plus miles, and it could carry two acoustic homing torpedoes. During the Vietnam War, a DASH was sometimes used to carry cameras for reconnaissance.

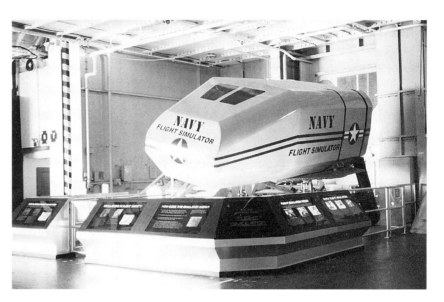

Navy flight simulator

Navy Flight Simulator

ON 15 MARCH 1997 Patriots Point held a ribbon cutting ceremony to signify the grand opening of a flight simulator. Visitors can experience five minutes of the Navy's air war over Iraq during the Persian Gulf War. Once in the simulator, the lights go down, the screen lights up and visitors are looking through the windshield of an F/A-18 Hornet fighter, rolling off the elevator on the aircraft carrier *Carl Vinson* (CV-70).

What follows are five minutes of fun as the theater simulates the dynamics of flight. During the flight the plane crosses the coastline, flies at a 90 degree bank angle down a canyon, launches missiles against Scud missiles, gets into a dogfight with a MiG, gets hit by a missile, and makes an emergency landing back on the carrier.

The simulator is actually a 15 seat enclosed theater that maneuvers on a set of hydraulic lifts. The script for the program running during the simulation was designed by aviators who served in Desert Storm. The voice-over is also that of a Desert Storm Pilot.

The simulator was built by Flight Avionics of North America, Orlando, Florida.

QH-50C

World War II Anti-aircraft Guns

THE MAJOR ANTI-AIRCRAFT GUNS used aboard U.S. Navy ships during World War II were the 5-inch dual purpose .38 gun, the 40mm Bofors, the 1.1 inch "Chicago Piano," and the 20mm Oerlikon cannon. Aboard *Yorktown* visitors will find all these weapons, although most are not located where they were installed during the war. Early in the war .50 caliber machine guns were aboard most ships, but within six months they had demonstrated an inability to knock down enemy planes at ranges that would preclude the plane from dropping its ordnance against the ship. No examples of World War II .50 caliber anti-aircraft guns are currently displayed within the museum.

Throughout World War II *Yorktown* carried twelve 5-inch guns. Two twin mounts existed fore and aft of the island, and four singles were mounted on the portside, two aft, and two forward near the number one elevator. The 5-inch guns usually opened fire first as they had a range of nearly 10 miles when aimed horizontally (elevated 45 degrees) and seven miles when firing vertically (elevated 85 degrees). The 5-inch guns were dual purpose, meaning they could fire at surface targets or aircraft. Usual rate of fire was 10 to15 rounds a minute. When World War II era Essex class carriers were modernized in the 1950s, the twin mounts forward and aft of the island were removed and two new mounts were added in new starboard sponsons. Later, others were removed from the portside. The four 5-inch guns currently aboard *Yorktown* show their final disposition. Aboard *Laffey*, the original six 5-inch guns in three mounts—two forward and one aft, have

5 inch gun

remained in position while the forward 5-inch gun aboard *Ingham* remains in its original location. The aft 5-inch gun aboard *Ingham* was removed soon after World War II.

The first intermediate range (4.2 miles at 41 degrees elevation) anti-aircraft gun aboard U.S. Navy ships was the six ton, 1.1 inch machine cannon that could fire up to 150 rounds per minute. By the end of the first year of the war, many 1.1s had been removed in favor of the more dependable and longer range 40mm Bofors guns. The 1.1" (28mm) shell did not explode and was capable of doing tremendous damage, but the major problem with the gun was its tendency to jam during battle. The 1.1" located on *Yorktown's* hangar deck is one of only three known examples still in existence. Perhaps the best moments for the 1.1" came during the Battle of the Eastern Solomons 24 August 1942 when the nine man crew 1.1's aboard the carrier *Enterprise* and the battleship *North Carolina* (BB-55) shot down a number of attacking planes.

When the 26 October 1942 Battle of Santa Cruz was fought, *Enterprise* and *South Dakota* (BB-57) were armed with the new liquid cooled 40mm Bofors. For that battle and those that followed throughout the war, the 40mm, which required 11 men to operate the quadruple mount, proved very effective. Range for the 40mm was six miles horizontally (42 degree elevation) and four miles vertically (90 degree elevation) although distance was affected by a fuse which detonated at two miles to prevent the shells from hitting other U.S. Navy ships. In air-sea battles—especially late in the war, the U.S. Navy kept ships in a close formation for more concentrated firepower, a

WORLD WAR II ANTI-AIRCRAFT GUNS

.50 caliber aircraft gun

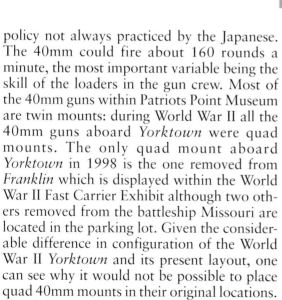

1.1" 'Chicago Piano' (bottom): 20mm AA gun (above)

40 mm AA gun mount removed from Franklin *(CV-13).*

policy not always practiced by the Japanese. The 40mm could fire about 160 rounds a minute, the most important variable being the skill of the loaders in the gun crew. Most of the 40mm guns within Patriots Point Museum are twin mounts: during World War II all the 40mm guns aboard *Yorktown* were quad mounts. The only quad mount aboard *Yorktown* in 1998 is the one removed from *Franklin* which is displayed within the World War II Fast Carrier Exhibit although two others removed from the battleship *Missouri* are located in the parking lot. Given the considerable difference in configuration of the World War II *Yorktown* and its present layout, one can see why it would not be possible to place quad 40mm mounts in their original locations.

The 20mm cannon with its crew of five appeared aboard U.S. Navy ships soon after

Pearl Harbor, and it was the last weapon to open fire on an enemy plane. Range against horizontal (35 degrees) targets was nearly three miles, effective range closer to one mile. Firing vertically (90 degrees), the 20mm shell carried nearly two miles but was effective at one half mile. Most 20mm guns, which could fire 450 rounds per minute with skilled canister loaders, were single mounts that fit conveniently wherever space permitted, However, when kamikaze attacks began in the fall of 1944, the need to gain more firepower led to 20mm twin mounts. The only 20mm gun within the museum is located above the 1.1 mount in the World War II Fast Carrier Exhibit.

Franklin *(CV-13) burning 19 March 1945* USN

Hancock *(CV-19) burns on 26 January 1945.* USN

5

Remembrance of Aircraft Carriers

BEGINNING SOON AFTER the end of World War II, the U.S. Navy began to dispose of its older aircraft carriers. Among the first to go was the oldest, *Saratoga* (CV-3), expended in the 1946 atom bomb tests at Bikini. *Independence* (CVL-22) survived the two explosions but was sunk after radiation tests were complete. The first carrier built from the keel up as an aircraft carrier in the U.S. Navy, *Ranger* (CV-4), was scrapped in 1947, and the most decorated carrier of the war, *Enterprise* (CV-6), followed in 1958. By 1979 most of the escort carriers were gone, all of the light fast carriers of the Independence class had been scrapped or transferred to foreign navies, and the long-serving carriers of the Essex class were rapidly being retired. As the Navy could not afford to maintain carriers past their useful life, dismantling was the only alternative. Fortunately, the veterans of the "Fighting Lady" and the Patriots Point staff recognized the need to provide exhibit space for carriers that were not preserved.

Veterans of the *Saratoga*, *Ticonderoga* (CV-14) and *Monterey* (CVL-26) were the first to accept the open invitation to establish memorial rooms in empty compartments aboard *Yorktown*. Many of *Yorktown's* compartments had been stripped after she was decommissioned in anticipation of dismantling. Consequently, the creation of exhibit rooms served not only to memorialize famous carriers but also to provide meaningful history in the empty compartments.

From 1979 to 1987 only the *Hancock* (CV-

19) and *Yorktown* (CV-5) veterans groups established "rooms" aboard *Yorktown* thereby leaving a considerable void both to visitors expecting to experience more World War II aircraft carrier history and to naval history itself. By 1987 it was apparent that not all veterans groups were as well established as others, and some groups had no artifacts or memorabilia to offer for the remembrance of their ships. Consequently, Patriots Point actively solicited carrier groups that did have meaningful artifacts and memorabilia to donate them to *Yorktown*. Within four years, *Enterprise*, *Essex* (CV-9), and *Franklin* (CV-13) had come aboard. To fill the void for the many other carriers, the Patriots Point staff created the World War II Fast Carrier Exhibit to honor all large, fast carriers (CV) and light fast carriers that won at least one battle star during World War II. The World War II Escort Carrier (CVE) Exhibit was created to honor all the small carriers and men who served aboard them. The "Naval Aviation in the Korean War Room" was established to honor all carriers with one or more battle stars for that conflict. In sum, the objective was to make the best effort possible to demonstrate to any aircraft carrier veteran who had experienced combat that he and his carrier had not been forgotten. The natural extension of this purpose led to the creation of the Super-carrier Exhibit.

In time, all veterans of aircraft carriers will join their ships on the high seas of history. Still, their children, and their children's children, will have a place aboard *Yorktown* to see deserving tribute paid.

World War II Fast Carrier Exhibit

As *Yorktown* (CV-10) traces her development and history to being one of the fast carriers built to lead United States forces across the Pacific to victory in World War II, it is only natural that an exhibit would be created to honor all the fast carriers that served. Too, it was the desire of Patriots Point that all veterans who served aboard fast carriers that won one or more battle stars, would be able to easily find aboard *Yorktown* an exhibit honoring them and their respective carrier.

The World War II fast carriers included the large fast carriers (CV like *Yorktown*) and the smaller, emergency fast carriers built on Cleveland class light cruiser hulls (CVL). When the war began for the United States on 7 December 1941, seven large fast carriers were in service (*Lexington* CV-2, *Saratoga* CV-3, *Ranger* CV-4, *Yorktown* CV-5, *Enterprise* CV-6, *Wasp* CV-7 and *Hornet* CV-8). On the first day of the war, six fast Japanese carriers demonstrated how much damage a carrier task force could deliver upon an opponent. Less than a year later, four United States Navy carriers had been lost (*Lexington* at Coral Sea, *Yorktown* at Midway, *Wasp* off Guadalcanal and *Hornet* off Santa Cruz), but as each had distinguished combat records, their names were perpetuated by trans-

World War II Fast Carrier Exhibit

NAVY CARRIERS

Development of the U.S. Navy's Aircraft Carriers to 1961

(This article by the author was originally published in Foundation—*Naval Aviation Museum Foundation, NAS Pensacola, 1990—and is reprinted here with modifications.)*

ALONG WITH NUCLEAR POWER, the major development in warfare during the first half of the 20th century was aviation. The advent of aviation totally changed the definition of sea power, as demonstrated during World War II and thereafter. An ancient proverb states that, "He who rules on the sea will very shortly rule on the land also." In the contemporary age, one must first control the air before taking control of the land and the sea.

Into the twilight of the 20th century, the aircraft carrier continues to demonstrate its value. In time of trouble or challenge, the aircraft carrier can (1) provide rapid response where the United States has no base rights or over-flight permission, (2) be ready for action upon arrival, (3) be self-sustaining during operations, (4) be elusive, (5) re-deploy, and (6) survive damage short of a nuclear blast.

The United States Navy's first significant experience with an airplane occurred on 14 November 1910 when civilian pilot Eugene Ely—wearing a football helmet and two bicycle innertubes for safety, flew off a makeshift flight deck temporarily built atop the cruiser *Birmingham* at Hampton Roads, Virginia. At San Francisco on 18 January 1911, Ely, his safety equipment now upgraded to motorcycle innertubes, made the first shipboard landing aboard a temporary deck built atop the cruiser *Pennsylvania*. The arresting gear for that first landing consisted of ropes and sandbags, a basic theoretical concept unchanged to this day.

NAVY CARRIERS

For much of the first half of the 20th century, the United States followed the lead of Great Britain in aircraft carrier development. During World War I, Britain built the first aircraft carrier, HMS *Argus*, on a merchant ship hull, setting precedent not only for the aircraft carrier but also for the use of merchant ship hulls for conversion to aircraft carriers (escort carriers). The HMS *Hermes* was the first carrier designed from the keel up as an aircraft carrier, but the Japanese commissioned their first designed-as-such carrier, IJN *Hosho*, a few weeks before the *Hermes* in 1923. British experiments with seaplanes demonstrated the reality that seaplanes were no match for land-based aircraft: therefore, the need to take state-of-the-art planes to sea.

On 20 March 1922, the U.S. Navy commissioned its first aircraft carrier, the USS *Langley* (CV-1), a former coal ship. Aboard *Langley*, the fundamental techniques of operating a carrier and its air group were developed.

Although Lieutenant T.G. Ellyson made the first catapult launch in 1912, that experience occurred on land. Ten years later on 18 November 1922, Lieutenant Kenneth Whiting made the first carrier catapult takeoff when launched from the *Langley*. Earlier on 26 October 1922, Lieutenant Commander Godfrey Chevalier had made the first carrier landing aboard *Langley*.

Just as the *Langley* was beginning her career, international politics intervened to directly affect the development of aircraft carriers and other capital ships in the world's major navies. The Washington Naval Treaty of 1922 and the later 1930 London Treaty limited carrier tonnage in the aggregate for respective navies and for individual ship types. Although common practice was to use the carrier in support of the battle fleet in scouting, attacking, and defending the battle line, a 1932 U.S. Navy fleet exercise attack on Pearl Har-

→

ferring them to new Essex class hulls under construction. None of the Essex class carriers, which first entered combat in late August 1943, were lost, but one of the wartime built CVLs of the Independence class was sunk in combat (*Princeton* CVL-23).

Representatives of all 30 fast carriers that won battle stars in World War II gathered aboard *Yorktown* on 7 December 1990, the 49th anniversary of the Pearl Harbor attack, to dedicate the new exhibit and reflect upon the history of the fast carrier "avengers." Among the speakers for the dedication were representatives of six carrier veterans groups who donated over $18,000 for the construction of the exhibit. The co-sponsors were *Enterprise*, *Essex* (CV-9), *Franklin* (CV-13), *Hancock* (CV-19), *Randolph* (CV-15) and *Wasp* (CV-18).

Located amidships on the hangar deck of *Yorktown*, each of the 30 carriers is honored with a large picture and engraved plaque displaying the carriers' war record. Among the more unique artifacts in the exhibit are: a 10 foot model of the *Franklin* as she looked after bomb damage that took nearly 800 lives; a 40mm gun mount removed from *Franklin* (Still showing some signs of battle damage, the mount was removed from *Franklin* when she returned to New York for repairs, was then used as a traveling display to help raise money for war bonds and was later given to an American Legion Post in Buffalo, New York, before being donated to Patriots Point for this exhibit.); the only known instrument to survive the sinking of the first *Hornet*; a lug with Japanese writing from the bomb that killed five on *Yorktown* (CV-10); one of only three known surviving 1.1" anti-aircraft gun mounts; and parts of the kamikazes that struck *Wasp*, *Randolph* and *Enterprise*.

Suspended above the WWII Fast Carrier Exhibit is a half-size model of an SBD "Dauntless" dive bomber, a carrier plane with a particularly distinguished combat record during World War II. The model was used in the filming of the television mini-series "War and Remembrance" that first aired in late 1988 and early 1989, and was donated to Patriots Point by ABC Circle Films.

FAST CARRIERS LOST IN WORLD WAR II

HORNET CV-8
LEXINGTON CV-2
PRINCETON CVL-23
WASP CV-7
YORKTOWN CV-5

FAST CARRIER BATTLE STAR TOTALS

ENTERPRISE CV-6	20
ESSEX CV-9	13
COWPENS CVL-25	12
YORKTOWN CV-10	11
BUNKER HILL CV-17	11
LEXINGTON CV-16	11
BELLEAU WOOD CVL-24	11
MONTEREY CVL-26	11
CABOT CVL-28	9
PRINCETON CVL-23	9
LANGLEY CVL-27	9
WASP CV-18	8
INDEPENDENCE CVL-22	8
HORNET CV-12	7
SARATOGA CV-3	7
SAN JACINTO CVL-30	7
BATAAN CVL-29	6
TICONDEROGA CV-14	5
INTREPID CV-11	5
HANCOCK CV-19	5
FRANKLIN CV-13	4
HORNET CV-8	4
YORKTOWN CV-5	3
RANDOLPH CV-15	3
BENNINGTON CV-20	3
WASP CV-7	2
LEXINGTON CV-2	2
RANGER CV-4	2
SHANGRI-LA CV-38	2
BON HOMME RICHARD CV-31	1

NAVY CARRIERS

bor demonstrated the potential of the carrier as a primary force rather than as a secondary or support force. The lesson of the 1932 Pearl Harbor fleet problem attack was not fully appreciated by the U.S. Navy, but it became the inspiration and example for the Japanese carrier force.

International treaties were not the only considerations in decisions of how to develop United States Navy carriers. Additionally significant was a decision to design carriers, like other warships, to have a beam measurement and configuration that would allow passage through the Panama Canal for quick transit from the Atlantic to the Pacific and vice versa.

A further decision in American carrier design was the option to defend against bombs with armor on the hangar deck and immediately above machinery spaces, with ordnance stowage deep in the hull. Although British carriers utilized armor on their flight decks rather extensively, the majority of American carriers built until the latter stages of World War II were designed to accept damage on wooden flight decks which could be rapidly repaired and vent concussion through the thin sides of the hangar deck and elevator wells. Penetration of an armored flight deck into a strongly built hangar could result in a warped flight deck almost impossible to repair in time to recover returning aircraft.

Although early American aircraft carriers were more than adequate for their aircraft, by the late 1930s it was evident that more consideration in carrier construction would have to be devoted to the requirements of newer, faster, and heavier aircraft. Until carriers could be built to accommodate needs of newer aircraft, planes would have to be subjected to construction constraints. Some planes transferred to Britain had squared wingtips to fit into 16 foot high hangar bays.

By 1942 the U.S. Navy could look upon its development of the aircraft carrier with a relative degree of satisfaction, but the period from

NAVY CARRIERS

1922 to 1942 is remembered as a time of research for the "ideal" carrier. Every design from the Navy's first carrier has had advantages and disadvantages. For the most part, succeeding designs addressed known problems.

The Navy's first carrier, *Langley*, was adequate for aircraft of the early and mid-1920s. Her greatest advantage, however, was a textbook example of what a carrier should not be. With a speed of only 14 knots, *Langley* was incapable of operating even with the slow battleships of the era, although she did participate in fleet exercises primarily for purposes of reconnaissance and spotting. With a small deck, little stowage, one elevator, and construction that could absorb little damage, *Langley* reverted to auxiliary status in 1936.

In late 1927 two battle cruiser hulls converted to aircraft carriers as a result of the Washington Naval Treaty were commissioned. *Saratoga* (CV-3) entered service one month before her sister, *Lexington* (CV-2), and these ships became the Navy's first fully operational aircraft carriers. For a little more than a decade, these two carriers were more than satisfactory for the aircraft that flew from their decks. *Lady Lex* and *Sara* were fast (34 knots), possessed large aircraft stowage, and had large flight decks. An unforeseen advantage in their turbo-electric machinery was the capability to supply a city with electric power. From 17 December 1929 until 16 January 1930, *Lexington* supplied Tacoma with four-and-one-quarter million kilowatt-hours when that city's power station broke down.

Despite their considerable favorable attributes, *Lexington* and *Saratoga* were not highly maneuverable, possessed relatively narrow hangar decks and low overheads, had only two elevators, and were poorly ventilated. Their tactical utilization was not well defined prior to World War II, as evidenced by retention of 8-inch guns until early 1942. Space used for these guns, their ordnance, and machinery

→

USS Saratoga *CV-3 Room*

CONVERTED FROM a battle-cruiser hull to an aircraft carrier as a result of the 1922 Washington Naval Conference, *Saratoga* (CV-3) was commissioned 16 November 1927. CV-3 and her sister ship, *Lexington* (CV-2), joined *Langley* (CV-1) to form the U.S. Navy's aircraft carrier force during the formative years of naval aviation. Many of the officers who served in top and mid-level posts during World War II gained relevant experience aboard *Saratoga* between 1927 and 1941, a contribution more valuable than the carrier's seven battle stars for World War II service.

Although big and fast, *Saratoga* was not very maneuverable. Hit twice by Japanese submarine torpedoes (11 January 1942 and 31 August 1942), she missed three of the four major carrier battles during the critical first year of the Pacific War. However, she was available for the 24 August 1942 Battle of the Eastern Solomons, and she enjoyed her most successful day in combat as her air group sank the Japanese light carrier, RYUJO. Severely damaged by kamikazes off Iwo Jima 21 February 1945, CV-3 was sunk during the Operation Crossroads atom bomb tests near Bikini on 25 July 1946.

On 8 April 1978, veterans of the *Saratoga* dedicated their museum room aboard *Yorktown*

View in Saratoga *(CV-3) Room*

in a second deck compartment originally used for berthing marines. Later, the exhibit expanded forward into a compartment which earlier served as Ready Room #4. Organized and built by CV-3's veterans, the exhibit follows an "open scrapbook" approach displaying a rich treasure of period artifacts, memorabilia, photographs and paper items. Artifacts removed from the carrier include pieces of the flight deck, a bridge voice tube cover, brass plates from the engine room, a clock from the Captain's office, the commissioning pennant, union jack, and two battle flags (one from the Guadalcanal campaign and one flown while off Iwo Jima).

Memorabilia displayed includes landing signal officers paddles, a bugle, pieces of kamikaze planes, the carrier's first newspaper dated 4 February 1928, and a pilot's flight helmet with goggles. Particularly significant are items donated by the families of Fleet Admiral William Halsey and Admiral Marc Mitscher. Halsey's summer flying jacket, naval aviator certificate and 5-star insignia on an overseas cap are displayed along with Mitscher's 2-star and 4-star flags and flight cap. Halsey served *Saratoga* as commanding officer (1935–37) and Mitscher served aboard in the late 1920s and 1930s as air officer and executive officer.

Among the many interesting photographs displayed are several showing the two torpedo hits (with 31 August 1942 damage report), her sinking off Bikini, dramatic kamikaze damage, construction, commissioning, and early air groups and aircraft. Also displayed are photos of all commanding officers including Halsey and John Towers. Admiral Towers later directed naval air during World War II.

USS Yorktown CV-5 Room

OVER HALF OF THE PEOPLE who visit Patriots Point were not born when World War II ended in 1945. Consequently, some visitors aboard *Yorktown* are surprised when they enter the Yorktown (CV-5) Room and find large newspaper and magazine articles displayed that feature stories and

---

NAVY CARRIERS

could have been much better used, and later was used in *Saratoga*, for aircraft fuel. Still, many design features of these ships, such as a closed bow, would return in later years and become standards in construction.

The first American carrier designed and built from the keel up as an aircraft carrier was *Ranger* (CV-4), commissioned in 1934. A design of many compromises, *Ranger* was a step forward in ventilation below decks and inside the hangar deck, but overall she was a disappointment. Although capable of 29 knots, she was not fast enough to outrun an enemy cruiser, or keep up with her own, was not good in Pacific swells, was not designed to take damage, was ill-armed, possessed inadequate armor, and did not have sufficient internal subdivision.

Despite all her shortcomings, six years later the Navy would build an "improved" *Ranger* due to treaty tonnage limitations. *Wasp* (CV-7) looked more like the members of the Yorktown class which immediately preceded her, but she was, in fact, a second *Ranger*. The *Wasp* was an improvement in terms of carrying a third elevator, which was the Navy's first deck-edge elevator.

Even before *Ranger* was commissioned in 1934, the Navy knew it would not meet its needs. In 1937 and 1938, the first two modern carriers were commissioned. These two ships, built side by side at Newport News, Virginia, profited from all the lessons learned to that point in time. Recipients of high praise in nearly all critical areas of design, *Yorktown* (CV-5) and *Enterprise* (CV-6) were the "Cadillac's" of aircraft carriers. Under construction for nearly four years, they were built with considerable attention to detail and the finest materials, such as stainless steel even for hand railings.

Fast (33 knots), maneuverable, stable, and capable of carrying and operating a large air group, the members of the Yorktown class had good internal subdivision to control flooding

NAVY CARRIERS

and good armor protection at the hangar deck level and above machinery spaces. Forerunner of the excellent Essex class design, the Yorktown class did have design flaws.

One design flaw was fatal to two of the three carriers of this class. The arrangement of boilers and engine rooms was such that a well-placed torpedo could cause a loss of power, thereby hindering the ship from pumping out water. At Midway in June 1942, *Yorktown* was badly damaged by bombs and torpedoes. Her internal subdivision design plan proved its worth by keeping the carrier afloat for two days despite a list of 26 degrees; however, the inability to restore power set her up as a perfect target for Japanese submarine torpedoes. Still, she was slow to die.

Four months later in October 1942, *Hornet* (CV-8) was lost in the Battle of Santa Cruz, again a victim of the boiler-engine room design and loss of power resulting from torpedo damage. Although not as critical to survival, the other major design disadvantage of the Yorktown class centered on an empty elevator well, or pit, in the middle of the hangar deck when the elevator was at flight deck level. Further, there was inadequate space for rapidly developing technology in communications, radar, and anti-aircraft fire control. Inadequate space for technological innovations, however, was a pervasive problem for most ships in the World War II era.

Although both her sisters were lost in battle, the third unit of the Yorktown class earned the distinction of earning more battle stars (20) than any other U.S. Navy ship to fight in World War II. *Enterprise* fought from Pearl Harbor to the shores of Japan, was awarded the first Presidential Unit Citation for carriers, and was, in the words of Secretary of the Navy James V. Forrestal, "the one ship that most nearly symbolizes the history of the United States In World War II."

→

Model and paintings in Yorktown *(CV-5) Room.*

pictures of *Yorktown* sinking. One headline reads "*Yorktown* SUNK," compelling visitors to study the exhibit for an explanation as to how the *Yorktown* was sunk but now rests in Charleston Harbor. Shortly, the visitor learns the articles refer to the **first** aircraft carrier named *Yorktown*.

The first *Yorktown* participated in the early Pacific raids in the Marshall and Gilbert Islands, and distinguished herself in the Battle of the Coral Sea and the Battle of Midway. *Yorktown* (CV-5) and *Lexington* (CV-2) flyers sank the Japanese carrier *Shoho* in the May 1942 Coral Sea battle.

In the Battle of Midway, *Yorktown* pilots sank the enemy carrier *Soryu* on the morning of 4 June 1942, and that afternoon a dozen of her pilots flew from the deck of sister ship *Enterprise* (CV-6) with pilots from the 'Big E' to destroy *Hiryu*. Planes from *Hiryu* earlier on 4 June disabled CV-5 with bombs and torpedoes. Struck by enemy submarine torpedoes on 6 June, "that gallant ship" *Yorktown* sank on 7 June 1942. Her name was perpetuated by the memorialized carrier, *Yorktown* (CV-10), which was commissioned in 1943.

The first *Yorktown* lived only five years, from 1937 to 1942. An effective ship thrown into desperate battles in the early days of World War II and subsequently lost, it was highly appropriate that her name was perpetuated by CV-10, later (and currently) as a guided missile cruiser.

The Yorktown (CV-5) Room is located on the gallery deck in what was the Flag Operations Center when CV-10 was last in commission. When CV-5 was sinking, no one was thinking about gathering souvenirs. Consequently, no artifacts from the carrier are on display. Memorabilia displayed includes a Navy Cross and Purple Heart with citations for Ensign Samuel J. Underhill who died while defending CV-5 in an SBD dive bomber during the Battle of the Coral Sea. Also displayed is a 52 inch model crafted by Harry Furlong of CV-5 as she appeared at the beginning of the war, and two large original paintings of the carrier by Diane Buchanan.

Portion of Enterprise (CV-6) Room.

USS Enterprise CV-6 Room

SHE RECEIVED 20 battle stars—more than any other ship of any type during World War II, was the first aircraft carrier to be awarded the Presidential Unit Citation, and was the only World War II fast carrier to receive both the Presidential Unit Citation and Navy Unit Commendation for that war. And of the six major carrier-versus-carrier battles of World War II, Enterprise fought in five and was steaming to the sixth as it ended.

On 23 April 1988 more than 250 veterans from the "Big E" gathered for the dedication of the Enterprise Room, which is located on the second deck of *Yorktown*. Taking advantage of the opportunity, the veterans also viewed a separate large exhibit honoring the "Big E" which

---

NAVY CARRIERS

Already designed before the attack on Pearl Harbor, the enlarged and improved Essex class carriers inspired by the three *Yorktowns* nevertheless did not arrive in the Pacific for combat until August 1943, over a year and a half after the American declaration of war.

Arrival in the Pacific of the large Essex class carriers and the smaller Independence class light carriers enabled the U.S. Navy to begin the uninterrupted offensive toward Japan. Big and fast, the Essex class carriers had a larger hangar deck (planes could now pass each other on the hangar deck), an amidships deck-edge elevator (which eliminated the open elevator well problem), and a larger flight deck. Further, the Essex and her sisters had good anti-torpedo protection, and the critical design flaw of the earlier Yorktown class was eliminated by alternating engine and boiler rooms. Although several units of the Essex class were badly damaged, including *Franklin* (CV-13), *Bunker Hill* (CV-17) and *Intrepid* (CV-11), none were sunk, and all but two of the 24 units served well into the postwar years.

The nine Independence class carriers were wartime emergency carriers built on Cleveland class light cruiser hulls. Advantages were the short amount of time required for conversion to carriers and their speed, which allowed them to operate with the larger fleet carriers. Disadvantages of the CVLs (light aircraft carriers) included smaller size and consequent smaller air group, small hangar, small island structure, short range in comparison with larger carriers, and a markedly higher accident rate in landing aircraft (smaller, therefore more pitch and roll).

Radar helped make possible the fast carrier task forces that overwhelmed Japanese island defenses throughout the Pacific. Radar provided early warning of air attack and enabled ships to keep place in formation regardless of weather or darkness. Further, radar meant that combat air patrol fighters need not be launched

NAVY CARRIERS

in great numbers until attack was imminent, the need for planes constantly airborne for early warning having been made unnecessary. Also, radar made possible the critical coordination from command to all ships via a combat information center.

A fast carrier force could take and control the air at the place of invasion. Task force organization allowed for a heavy concentration of anti-aircraft defense and submarine and aircraft protection as fewer ships and planes could offer greater protection. Japanese battle strategy usually did not reflect this tactical theory or implementation. When under attack, Japanese ships usually went in all directions rather than keeping close formation.

Constantly in combat from the first days of the war, fast carriers were highly mobile, and their ability to hit targets 1,000 miles apart in a 24-hour period kept the Japanese off guard. At the loss of four large carriers, one light fleet carrier, and over 5,000 officers and men, U.S. Navy carrier planes sank 161 Japanese warships and 359 merchant vessels, and destroyed 12,000 Japanese planes in the air and on the ground.

Reality is that some ships are glamorous and some are not. Escort carriers were perhaps the least glamorous. They did not look powerful, were not fast, and many were never intended to be warships when they were first built. Still, escort carriers steamed away from World War II with more battle stars than all the fast carriers combined, more Presidential Unit Citations, and more Navy Unit Commendations. Granted, there were more escort carriers than fast carriers but, as a group, they were nearly as late as the Essex and Independence carriers in getting into the war. Once there, however, they performed beyond expectations and played an extremely significant role in winning the war in both the Pacific and the Atlantic.

→

was later shipped to the Bremerton Naval Museum in Bremerton, Washington.

Included in the Enterprise Room are large photographs tracing the history of the ship from her pre-war days through the Battle of Midway (where planes flying from her deck sank three of the four Japanese carriers lost), the Battle of the Eastern Solomons, Battle of Santa Cruz, Battle of the Philippine Sea and Battle of Leyte Gulf. Among the artifacts and memorabilia presented in display cases are: pieces of the last of several kamikaze planes that crashed into the carrier; a shrapnel pierced helmet worn by Marine Joe Markowitz (the shrapnel is still in his forehead); a 52 inch scratch-built model of the carrier; air group insignia for all the air groups that served aboard; pieces of the flight deck; signal flags; uniform parts; a one-cell flashlight; 40mm shell casing; art prints; and models of planes that flew from the carrier during her nine year operational life.

Although declared in 1945 "The one ship that most nearly symbolizes the history of the United States Navy in World War II" by Secretary of the Navy James V. Forrestal, the ship was sold in 1958 and dismantled. However, she still lives in naval literature, and at Patriots Point and the several other major exhibits in museums placed in her memory.

USS Essex *CV-9 Room*

EARLY IN WORLD WAR II, no single hull was awaited with more eagerness and interest than *Essex* (CV-9). Servicemen watched news releases and the horizon for the approach of the carrier that would give her name to the aircraft carrier class that would prove successful in combat and offer a highly adaptable design. Essex-class carriers were eminently successful in World War II and in two subsequent wars. Commissioned on the last day of 1942, *Essex* fought her way across the Pacific—often alongside *Yorktown*—and won the Presidential Unit Citation and 13 battle stars (second only to *Enterprise* CV-6 which won 20).

Following victory in World War II, *Essex*

In-board view of Essex *(CV-9) Room.*

was decommissioned in January 1947. Recommissioned 15 January 195l, she looked slightly different with a streamlined island superstructure. Soon thereafter, the carrier began the first of three tours during the Korean War. The first carrier to launch jet fighters on combat missions, *Essex* received 4 battle stars and the Navy Unit Commendation for Korean War service. Modernized with an angled flight deck and other changes in 1955, she served until finally decommissioned in 1970.

Although the *Essex* was scraped, a few pieces of the ship were saved. Nearly all surviving artifacts are on display aboard sister ship *Yorktown*. On Flag Day 14 June 1989, Patriots Point Naval and Maritime Museum staff joined with veterans of the *Essex* to dedicate a permanent memorial to CV-9. The compartment selected was *Yorktown's* parachute drying room. Like most carrier exhibits, the Essex Room features a photographic history of the ship, many enclosed in large 4×8 foot letter display cases that spell *Essex*.

Significant artifacts on display directly from the *Essex* include a binnacle, compass stand, repeater compass, voice tube, valve wheel, commissioning pennant and a 1942 "state of the art" ship's telephone which served hangar deck control. Memorabilia donated by *Essex* veterans include parts of the 25 November 1944 kamikaze that crashed the carrier killing 15, a por-

NAVY CARRIERS

Before the Casablanca and Commencement Bay class escort carriers were designed and built from the keel up as such, escort carriers were originally merchant ships or tankers such as those of the Sangamon class. Top speed was not over 20 knots with a trailing wind, smooth seas, and the Japanese Navy in hot pursuit.

Even though escort carriers were not expected to withstand significant damage, several took serious hits and survived. Too often, however, the thin skins of the escort carriers were not equal to the punishment inflicted. Perhaps it is surprising that only six were lost. Five of the six that were lost did share at least one characteristic with the five fleet carriers that went down. Specifically, they got in major blows against the enemy before being lost.

The U.S. Navy's escort carriers in World War II served in a multitude of roles, including the unenviable but necessary functions of training and plane transport. Early in the war while the carrier shortage was critical, a few escort carriers were ordered to serve operationally. These were so successful in combat air patrol, attack, observation, invasion support, pre-invasion strikes, and close air support that escort carriers would continue to be used in some of these functions not only throughout the remainder of World War II but also into the Korean War.

While every function imaginable was assigned to escort carriers in the Pacific, the major function of escort carriers in the Atlantic was antisubmarine duty. The hunter-killer groups composed of escort carriers, destroyers, and destroyer escorts completely turned around the war in the Atlantic. Although their strategic role was defensive (to protect convoys), their tactical approach was offensive. U.S. Navy hunter-killer groups were responsible for 65 percent of the American effort.

Several U.S. Navy escort carriers experienced particularly noteworthy successes in the Atlantic. Among these was *Bogue* (CVE-9),

NAVY CARRIERS

one of the U.S. Navy pioneers of the hunter-killer groups, responsible for the sinking of 13 German submarines, sunk either by her or by her escorts (eight by planes, two shared with her escorts, and three by escorts alone). *Card* (CVE-11) had an equally impressive record, and *Guadalcanal* (CVE-60), which captured *U-505* and brought her home as a prize, will be long remembered. The German submarine *U-505* still exists and is on display at the Chicago Museum of Science and Industry.

After World War II, many escort carriers were broken up, sold to other countries, or returned to the Maritime Commission to be reconverted. Some, however, served on into Korea, but none survives today.

In the fall of 1945, just as World War II ended, the Navy commissioned the first two of the three Midway class battle-carriers. *Midway* (CVB-41), *Franklin D. Roosevelt* (CVB-42) and *Coral Sea* (CVB-43) had considerable advantages over contemporary Essex class carriers with their armored flight deck, removal of most anti-aircraft batteries to the hangar deck level, larger hangar deck and flight deck, capacity to operate 150 planes (which proved impractical), and more anti-aircraft guns. The disadvantages of the Midway class carriers were their inability to transit the Panama Canal due to their increased beam, their high cost, and later, the high cost of modernization. None of the three Midway class ships ever saw battle in their original configuration. Within a few years of their commissioning, these carriers underwent the first in a series of modifications that enabled them to serve for nearly a half century.

Before the end of World War II, Germany introduced jet aircraft into combat. In 1945 the Ryan FR-1 Fireball, a hybrid prop-jet, became the first jet in American carrier aviation. Other jets would serve the U.S. Navy in the transition from propeller to jet propul-

→

tion of the Japanese pilot's parachute, a World War II era life jacket and survival kit, a portion of the World War II homeward-bound pennant, an article and photographs of Commander David McCampbell (the leading U.S. Navy ace with 34 kills), a copy of a 1966 signed photograph from actress Natalie Wood, a recommissioning invitation, and the medals of Vice Admiral R.A. Ofstie (commanding officer 1943–44) which include the Navy Cross, Distinguished Service Medal, Silver Star and Legion of Merit among others. Patriots Point designed the exhibit, obtained a 42 inch model from the Buffalo & Erie County Naval & Servicemen's Park and provided all text-plates including the listing of CV-9's commanding officers, battle stars and air groups.

USS Franklin *CV-13 Room*

THE ONLY MAJOR memorial exhibit honoring the famous World War II aircraft carrier *Franklin* (CV-13) was dedicated on 17 March 1990 at Patriots Point Museum. Ceremonies for the carrier that suffered more casualties and more combat damage than any other U.S. Navy carrier to return to port during World War II were held on the hangar deck of the *Yorktown*, which is a sister ship of the *Franklin*.

Affectionately nicknamed "Big Ben," the *Franklin* lost 724 men in addition to hundreds wounded when she was hit by two bombs on 19 March 1945while operating only 50 miles off Kyushu, Japan's southernmost island. The number of men killed aboard *Franklin* on that one day surpassed the total number of men lost on all four of the large U.S. Navy fast carriers lost in 1942. On 30 October 1944, 56 men died on "Big Ben" when she was hit by a kamikaze off the Philippines.

The dedication of the Franklin Room was originally planned for October 1989, but had to be rescheduled due to the 21–22 September 1989 hurricane. The new date chosen was intended to coincide with the 45th anniversary of the ship's most traumatic moments.

Over 400 attended the dedication ceremo-

Ten foot model of Franklin *as she looked on 20 March 1945.*

nies aboard the *Yorktown.* Among the guests were several widows of *Franklin* crewmen including one who lost her husband on 19 March 1945, never remarried and dedicated herself to assisting in the placement of memorials for her late husband and others who died in the service of the United States. For all guests the dedication on the *Yorktown's* hangar deck was a poignant experience as approximately half the men lost aboard "Big Ben" in 1945 died in the hangar deck.

Not all the artifacts from the *Franklin*—which was scrapped in 1968—are in the second deck

NAVY CARRIERS

sion with the Grumman F9F Panther becoming the first Navy jet to enter combat. For jets to be effective, though, extensive changes would have to be made to the carriers that would take them into combat. Jet aircraft were considerably heavier than prop planes: attack planes would weigh several times more than their World War II counterparts. This fact alone required carriers to have stronger flight decks and greatly improved catapult systems. Jets required more fuel than propeller aircraft, with a subsidiary need for larger and faster fuel pumps. Also, larger and higher capacity elevators were needed for both the new jet planes and their ordnance.

The outbreak of the Korean War spurred modernization of the nearly two dozen Essex class carriers then operational or in mothballs. Whereas the three Midways could operate jets in their original configuration, the Essex class carriers were limited. Throughout the postwar period, the U.S. Navy's Ship Characteristics Board (SCB) supervised the fleet carrier conversion program. Although not all Essex class carriers were modernized to the same degree in the nine-month to two-year yard periods, many were upgraded to effectively operate early jet planes.

Modernization of the Essex class carriers would not only address the basic changes necessary to operate jet aircraft, but would also address other known deficiencies in ship design and personnel needs. Flight decks were strengthened to handle heavier planes landing at higher speeds. Higher capacity hydraulic catapults were installed with a few units receiving the even stronger steam catapult to propel heavier jets. Catapult blast detectors were also added to protect personnel and other aircraft.

Again following the lead of British innovation, the Essex class carrier *Antietam* (CV-36) was modified with an experimental angled flight deck to separate takeoff and landing areas. The merits of the angled flight deck were quickly obvious for safety and the ability of planes to be landing while others were launching. Contemporary with the introduction of the angled deck was the mirror landing system—a set of colored lights that, rather than the long-used LSO or Landing Signal Officer, would guide a pilot onto the flight deck—and stronger arresting gear and improved attendant machinery to better serve the demands of jet aircraft.

During modernization, the aft or number three elevator of Essex class carriers was moved from inside the ship to an outboard position starboard, thereby giving these carriers a second deck-edge elevator and eliminating the void created in the hangar deck when the aft elevator was at flight deck level. The flight deck was growing in size due to the angle deck and second deck-edge elevator, and seemed to grow larger with the removal of 5-inch anti-aircraft guns from the flight deck fore and aft of the island: 40mm guns were removed in favor of the newer 3-inch guns.

Modernization almost completely changed the appearance of the island structure of Essex class carriers. Anti-aircraft guns were removed, the stack was angled aft, the original tripod mast was replaced by a stronger pole mast to support newer communications and radar equipment, and the bridge was enclosed. On the lower starboard side of the island, an escalator was installed to quickly move aircrew from their relocated and better protected ready rooms to the flight deck.

Another change during modernization was a return to the enclosed bow originally featured in the designs of the first *Lexington* and *Saratoga*. Three Essex class carriers had their forward flight decks destroyed in heavy seas, thereby inspiring the "hurricane bow" nickname. The enclosed bow, angle deck, improved fire and splinter curtains, along with other additions and modifications, raised the displacement weight of modernized Essex class carriers from their original 27,000 tons to 36,000 plus →

"BIG" and "BEN" display cases contain artifacts, memorabilia and pictures in the Franklin *Room.*

compartment housing the memorial exhibit. The largest artifact, a 40mm quad gun mount, is on *Yorktown's* hangar deck in the World War II Fast Carrier exhibit along with a 10 foot model of the carrier as she appeared the day after being damaged in the 1945 attack. Other especially notable artifacts (some placed in cases built to spell BIG BEN) include a torn and burned battle flag flown on 19 March 1945; a partially burned Order-of-the-Day for that terrible date; several pieces of steel and wood from the carrier, and personal memorabilia of the two officers, Father Joseph T. O'Callahan and Lt. Donald Gary, who were awarded the Medal of Honor for their heroic actions aboard *Franklin* off the coast of Japan.

USS Ticonderoga *CV-14 Room*

COMMISSIONED 8 May 1944, *Ticonderoga* (CV-14) arrived in the Pacific too late for action in any of the six major carrier battles. However, she did arrive in time to win five battle stars for air operations ranging from the Philippines to the Japanese home islands. Seriously damaged by kamikazes 21 January 1945, the carrier was out of action for repairs until April but operated continuously upon return until the war ended in August. Decommissioned 29 June 1946

In-board view of Ticonderoga (CV-14) Room.

along with most of her sister ships, the ship rested in mothballs until commissioned again 11 September 1954. The carrier returned to duty too late for action off Korea, but her air group was among the first to fly in the Vietnam War. Serving as an attack carrier (CVA), "*Tico*" was deployed off Vietnam between 1964 and late 1969. Away from the conflict only for repairs and training, the carrier and her air groups earned three Navy Unit Commendations for operations off and over Vietnam. Converted to an antisubmarine carrier (CVS) in 1970, the carrier returned to the Pacific. Before being decommissioned for the last time on 16 November 1973, *Ticonderoga* participated in the recovery of the astronauts and capsule for the Apollo 16 mission in April 1972 and for the Apollo 17 mission in December 1972.

After the carrier was scrapped, many of her artifacts were shipped to a museum in Ticonderoga, New York. On 6 May 1979, veterans of the *Ticonderoga* dedicated another exhibit aboard *Yorktown* in a second deck compartment that originally served as the gunnery department office. Currently on display in the Ticonderoga Room are three large brass plaques, a deck clock and decking, all removed from the carrier. Also displayed are pieces of the kamikaze planes that struck the ship and a 56 inch model of *Ticonderoga* in her final configuration. Primarily a photographic history, the exhibit features photographs of earlier vessels

tons in some units. To compensate for this additional weight, and particularly the additional top-weight, a blister was added to the hull of these ships. The blister not only aided in stability but also provided additional fuel stowage and better torpedo defense.

Personnel needs are considered in the design of carriers, but overcrowding has been a perennial problem. Overcrowding was particularly acute during World War II when unforeseen additions of anti-aircraft guns, radar, and communications poured more men than originally expected into living spaces.

Although some Essex class carriers would remain as attack carriers into the Vietnam War, others would be utilized as antisubmarine carriers. The addition of the helicopter to the fleet in 1948 enhanced both antisubmarine effectiveness and rescue work. In later years, helicopters would transport troops into battle. Ships used for this purpose would include converted escort carriers as well as a few *Essexes*. In 1961 Iwo Jima class amphibious assault ships began to fill this role. About the same tonnage as the Yorktown class carriers, the Iwo Jima class helicopter carriers also strongly resemble their famous predecessors.

In the 1950s and 1960s, while Essex and Midway class carriers were being modernized, new "super-carriers" of the Forrestal class were being built in response to new concepts and roles. Completed between 1955 and 1968, the eight oil fueled carriers (four Forrestal class carriers and four Kitty Hawk class carriers) were larger than earlier carriers at nearly 80,000 tons, had four elevators (all deck edge), featured a well arranged island, and could operate heavy aircraft with nuclear capacity (the Midway class could operate the same aircraft). Originally believed to have a service life of approximately 30 years, the carriers of the Forrestal and Kitty Hawk classes will have had at least 15 years added as a result of service life extension programs. Unlike the major upgrading programs applied to the Essex and Midway classes, programs for the Forrestal and Kitty Hawk classes were essentially rehabilitation and reconditioning agendas. While upgrades do occur in missile defense systems, communications, and radar, the major service life extension programs center on reconditioning main and auxiliary machinery and replacing firemains, plumbing, wiring and circuits.

Before the last unit of the Forrestal and Kitty Hawk carriers was commissioned in 1968, the U.S. Navy's first nuclear powered carrier was built and placed in service in late 1961. The *Enterprise* (CVN-65) could steam over 200,000miles before having to refuel her eight nuclear reactors. Faster than any other earlier carrier, *Enterprise* offered great endurance, capacity to carry a larger stowage of aviation fuel, more ordnance, and a lack of stack exhaust which eliminated "ramp burble," or turbulence for aircraft approaching touchdown on deck.

The nuclear carriers that have entered service since *Enterprise* carry fewer reactors (only two in *Nimitz*) and can operate 13 years before refueling. Although missiles have replaced guns as the primary anti-aircraft defense and computers have facilitated nearly all phases of carrier operations, the basic functions, purpose-in-being, and modus operandi of the aircraft carrier have essentially remained the same since the early 1960s.

Prior to World War II the aircraft carrier served primarily as a means of defending the battle fleet. During World War II the carrier developed into the supreme offensive capital ship and has since become the major platform for the projection of diplomatic policy. The devastating power of the aircraft carrier has been demonstrated tactically and strategically on numerous occasions in the last 50 years. Hopefully, this power will not be seriously challenged again.

named Ticonderoga, construction and commissioning of CV-14, air operations against Japanese targets, kamikaze damage, service as an antisubmarine carrier, Vietnam era attack carrier, and the recovery mission for the Apollo program. One panel features commissioning day pictures for the contemporary guided missile cruiser *Ticonderoga* (CG47).

USS Hancock *CV-19 Room*

COMMISSIONED 15 April l944 and first available for combat in early October 1944, the *Hancock* (CV-19) received five hard-earned battle stars during the final year of the Pacific war. As the U.S. Navy neared the Philippines and the Japanese homeland, the intrinsic advantage of interior lines made the carrier advance even more dangerous. Constantly under threat of air attack from enemy land bases, new carriers in the combat zone had to be immediately effective. *Hancock* gave better than she got although the carrier suffered major damage due to a flight deck landing accident on 26 January 1945 that killed 50, and a kamikaze crash on 7 April 1945 that killed 62. *Hancock* air groups delivered crushing blows to enemy forces in the Philippines, Indochina, Okinawa, and the Japanese home islands.

Inactivated after the war, the carrier was moved from the mothball fleet at Bremerton, Washington, modernized and classified CVA (attack aircraft carrier as opposed to CVS—antisubmarine aircraft carrier) on 1 October 1952. Although activated in response to the Korean War, "*Hanna*" did not serve off Korea. In 1956 the carrier was again modernized, receiving an angled flight deck and other significant changes. The first carrier to operate steam catapults, *Hancock* demonstrated the value of the more powerful launching machinery. One of the first carriers to participate in the Vietnam War, *Hancock* was awarded a Navy Unit Commendation to complement another such award for her performance during World War II.

Decommissioned 30 January 1976 after 32

years of service, the carrier was scrapped. However, by 1976 considerable interest attended the preservation of World War II ships and part of the island structure from *Hancock* was integrated into a major exhibit within the National Air and Space Museum in Washington, DC. Other artifacts were available for a large exhibit aboard *Yorktown*, and on 28 September 1984 the Hancock CV/CVA-19 Room was dedicated by the Hancock Veterans Association and Patriots Point staff.

Monterey (CVL-26) Ready Room aboard Yorktown.

Two compartments on the gallery deck were available to house *Hancock* artifacts. The former radio transmitter room was used to display the carrier's World War II history, and the former air operations office was prepared for display of the carrier's Cold War and Vietnam history. Artifacts removed from the ship include planking from the original flight deck, an emergency light, two voice tubes, the carrier's decorations and campaign ribbons board, a large bronze plaque dated 1946 recording World War II campaigns and engagements, 1959 and 1969 Pacific Fleet battle efficiency plaques, and 1971 and 1972 Flatley memorial awards for naval aviation safety. The large veterans memorabilia donations include uniforms and pieces of the 7 April 1945 kamikaze hit. Pilot memorabilia includes a navigational plotting board, oxygen mask, goggles, boots, flight suit, flight jacket parachute harness, cloth survival charts and maps, and survival kit among other items.

USS Monterey CVL-26 Room

ALTHOUGH ALL NINE light fast carriers of the Independence class are represented in Patriots Point's World War II Fast Carrier Exhibit, the veterans of only one, *Monterey* (CVL-26), established a museum room aboard *Yorktown* (1978). Commissioned 17 June 1943, the 11,000-ton *Monterey* earned 11 battle stars during the last two years of World War II. Decommissioned 11 February 1947, the carrier was recommissioned 15 September 1950 in response to the Korean War. *Monterey* did not serve off Korea but instead became the Navy's training carrier based at NAS Pensacola for four years before final decommissioning 16 January 1956. The carrier was scrapped in 1971.

In March 1942 the U.S. Navy ordered nine Cleveland class cruiser hulls converted into "emergency" fast carriers. With a speed of 31 plus knots, the nine Independence class light carriers steamed in formation with the larger Essex class carriers to lead the advance across the Pacific toward Japan. Common practice was to include two Essex class and one or two Independence class carriers in the same task group. Occasionally classified with escort carriers in contemporary articles, the CVLs officially and operationally were "fleet" carriers. Only *Bataan* (CVL-29) served off Korea.

Utilizing a second deck compartment which once served *Yorktown* as Squadron Ready Room #3, the Monterey Room is divided in two sections and features four separate segments of the carrier's life. The Monterey Memorial Ready Room displays 15 ready room chairs and equipment germane to air operations. Although the chairs and equipment are all original *Yorktown* artifacts, the large photographs display air operations aboard *Monterey*.

At the rear of the ready room is a display of Torpedo Squadron 34 (VT-34) pictures and memorabilia. Included are cloth maps of Japan, a flight jacket with period "Vargas Girl" rendering, and a copy of the last air operations schedule for the squadron dated 15 August 1945. VT-34 was approaching Japan on a mission when word came that the war was over.

World War II Escort Carriers Exhibit.

The portside of the compartment is divided into a display honoring two *Monterey* veterans who later became famous, and an expansive photographic display depicting the life of the carrier. Former *Monterey* gunnery officer and assistant navigator Gerald R. Ford became the 38th President of the United States, and Thomas S. Gates became Secretary of the Navy. Displayed with the photographs of the carrier are a piece of flight deck planking from CVL-26, a flag, and a clock from one of the carrier's F6F Hellcats. Also displayed is a panel honoring the contemporary cruiser *Monterey* (CG-61) which was commissioned 16 June 1990.

World War II Escort Carrier Exhibit

Opened in February 1990, the World War II Escort Carrier Exhibit honors the escort carriers (CVE) that fought in both the Atlantic and Pacific. Sponsored by Patriots Point Museum, the exhibit is located on the second deck of *Yorktown*.

Included in the exhibit a visitor will find a five foot Casablanca class model; art prints of *Gambier Bay* (CVE-73), *St. Lo* (CVE-63) and *White Plains* (CVE-66); a 4'×8' diorama of the

Battle off Samar; a search light from *Card* (CVE-11) and significant artifacts and memorabilia from *Fanshaw Bay* (CVE-70), *Bogue* (CVE-9) and other famous escort carriers.

The U.S. Navy's escort carriers in World War II served in a multitude of roles including the unenviable but necessary functions of training and plane transport. Early in the war while the carrier shortage was critical, escort carriers were ordered to serve operationally. So successful in combat air patrol, attack, observation, invasion support, pre-invasion strikes and close air support, escort carriers continued to be used in many of these functions throughout World War II and in some off Korea.

While every function imaginable was assigned to escort carriers in the Pacific, their major function in the Atlantic was antisubmarine duty. The hunter-killer groups of escort carriers, destroyers and destroyer-escorts completely reversed Allied fortunes in the Atlantic and played no small role in ultimate victory.

The first escort carrier was the *Long Island* (CVE-1), converted from a merchant ship in 1941. *Charger* (CVE-30) was the other member of the Long Island class. Also converted from merchant hulls was the Bogue class (10 carriers completed in 1942–43) while the four ships of the Sangamon class were converted from tankers in 1942. The first escort carriers designed as such were the 50 units of the Casablanca class completed in 1943–44 with all earlier experience resulting in the 1944–46 construction of the 19 Commencement Bay class escort carriers.

The overall length of World War II escort carriers ranged from 492 feet (*Long Island*) to 557 feet (Commencement Bay class); full load displacement from 10,982 (Casablanca class) to 24,100 (Commencement Bay class); speed ranged from 17 to 19 knots and aircraft complement ranged from 28 to 33 for operating purposes. Ship's company numbered 920: air groups numbered from 100 to 150. Armor protection was used sparingly if at all, one 5 inch gun was the heaviest weapon aboard most escort carriers but 40mm and 20mm guns were mounted extensively, usually about sixteen 40mm barrels and twenty 20mm.

Among popular misconceptions is the belief that the CVLs of the Independence class were escort carriers. They were not. The nine CVLs were converted from Cleveland class light cruiser hulls to serve as fast carriers (speeds up to 30 knots) and their utilization was separate from escort carriers. Another misconception was that the two Great Lakes paddle steamers converted to training carriers (*Wolverine* IX 64 and *Sable* IX-81) were escort carriers: again, they were not.

Even though escort carriers were not expected to withstand significant damage, several took serious hits and survived. Too often, however, the thin skins of the escort carriers were not equal to the punishment inflicted. Six CVEs did not survive the war. *Liscome Bay* (CVE-56) was lost within three days of her first combat mission; the 646 lives lost when she was torpedoed off the Gilbert Islands ranked her second only to *Franklin's* losses. *Block Island* (CVE-21), the only CVE lost in the Atlantic, accounted for two German submarines with her own planes while her escorts sank five including *U-549*, the submarine that placed the fatal torpedoes into her. *Gambier Bay* and *St.Lo* were lost off Samar during the Battle of Leyte Gulf; *Gambier Bay* sank as a result of gunfire while *St. Lo* was lost later on that same day after being hit by a kamikaze. *Ommaney Bay* (CVE-79) was sunk by a kamikaze off the Philippines 4 January 1945, and *Bismarck Sea* (CVE-95) was sunk by kamikazes off Iwo Jima 21 February 1945.

The majority of German submarines lost in World War II were accounted for by the British. Twenty-three percent of the German submarines destroyed were accounted for by American forces with U.S. Navy hunter-killer groups responsible for 65 percent of the American effort.

Several U.S. Navy escort carriers experienced particularly noteworthy successes in the Atlantic. Among these were *Bogue*, one of the U.S. Navy pioneers of the hunter-killer groups, responsible for 13 German submarines sunk by her or her escorts (eight by planes, two shared with her escorts and three by escorts alone; *Card* which scored eight sub kills with her escorts; and *Guadalcanal* (CVE-60) which captured *U-505* and brought her home as a prize. In the Pacific, *Anzio* (CVE-57) totaled five Japanese submarines with her planes and escorts.

Escort Carriers Lost in World War II

Block Island CVE-21
Bismarck Sea CVE-95
Gambier Bay CVE-73
Liscome Bay CVE-56
Ommaney Bay CVE-79
St. Lo CVE-63

Escort Carrier Battle Star Leaders

Suwannee CVE-26		13
Chenango CVE-28		11
Santee CVE-29		9
Anzio CVE-57		9

World War II Carrier Presidential Unit Citation Exhibit

Dedicated 8 October 1988, the World War II Carrier Presidential Unit Citation Exhibit honors the 25 aircraft carriers awarded the highest medal awarded to combat ships. Co-sponsored by the veterans of the *Yorktown* (CV-10), *Belleau Wood* (CVL-24) and *Gambier Bay* (CVE-73), the exhibit is located on the hangar deck of *Yorktown*. Each of the 25 carriers was represented during the ceremony at which time the citations for each award were read and the veterans of each carrier recognized.

The six large fast carriers to receive the Presidential Unit Citation during World War II were *Enterprise* CV-6 (the first ship ever to receive the award), *Essex* (CV-9), *Lexington* (CV-16), *Franklin* (CV-13), *Hornet* (CV-12) and *Yorktown* (CV-10).

Presidential Unit Citation Exhibit

The three light fast carriers to receive the award were *Belleau Wood* (CVL-24), *Cabot* (CVL-28) and *San Jacinto* (CVL-30).

Sixteen escort carriers received the Presidential Unit Citation for World War II combat. They were *Fanshaw Bay* CVE-70 (one individual award and one unit award), *Gambier Bay* (CVE-73), *Kalinin Bay* (CVE-68), *Kitkun Bay* (CVE-71), *St. Lo* (CVE-63), *White Plains* (CVE-66), *Card* (CVE-11), *Guadalcanal* (CVE-60), *Bogue* (CVE-9), *Lunga Point* (CVE-94), *Natoma Bay* (CVE-62), *Petrof Bay* (CVE-80), *Sangamon* (CVE-26), *Santee* (CVE-29), *Savo Island* (CVE-78) and *Suwannee* (CVE-27).

Artifact and memorabilia contributions were made by the three sponsors, plus *Fanshaw Bay* (commissioning pennant), *Bunker Hill* (CV-17) and *Enterprise* (CV-6) veterans. Original artwork for the exhibit was contributed by the late noted naval artist, Joe Cason.

Midway Class Carrier Room

DESIGNED AS BATTLE-CARRIERS during World War II, the three units of the Midway class (*Midway* CV-41, commissioned 10 September 1945; *Franklin D. Roosevelt* CV-42, commissioned 27

October 1945; and *Coral Sea* CV-43, commissioned 1 October 1947) were not commissioned in time to see combat in that war. Although available during the Korean War, all three operated in Atlantic and Mediterranean waters instead of the Pacific. Continuously at sea during most of the Cold War years, all three served off Vietnam with distinction. *Coral Sea* participated in the 1986 strike on Libya, and *Midway* launched strikes during the Persian Gulf war. FDR was sold in 1977 and *Coral Sea* was sold in 1991 (scrapping began in Baltimore, Maryland, in 1993 but the process is not expected to be completed until sometime in 1998 in India). At the time of this writing, plans are going forward to preserve *Midway* as a museum in San Diego.

The Midway Class Carrier Room aboard *Yorktown* is located on the second deck in a compartment that once served as the EAM Key Punch Room. 1960-era computers and electronic data processing equipment are still on display. Primarily a photographic display depicting the service life of the three carriers, the exhibit displays three individual bronze plaques listing pilots and aircrew lost during the Vietnam War, a plaque listing *Coral Sea* commanding officers, and cruise books. An original painting by David Clark honoring *Coral Sea* is also displayed. The exhibit was opened in 1991 and is sponsored by the Coral

Super-Carriers Exhibit

Sea Association and Patriots Point in honor of the three ships and all the men who served aboard.

When first completed as battle-carriers (CVB), the ships were 968 feet long, displaced 58,600 tons and carried 18 five inch guns and 100 40mm barrels. Entering service just as the jet age dawned, the Midway's were very well suited for conversion. Already possessing a steel flight deck, angled decks and many other modifications were made during several modernization yard visits. In final configuration the *Midway* was 1,001 feet long and displaced over 64,000 tons. Modifications decreased speed from 33 knots to 29.5 knots, but the loss in speed did not adversely affect the Cold War mission of the carriers.

Super-Carriers

OVER 200 VETERANS of the world's first nuclear aircraft carrier, *Enterprise* CVAN-65, assembled at Patriots Point on 18 August 1992 to help dedicate a new Super-Carrier exhibit. Located on *Yorktown's* hangar deck immediately forward of the World War II Fast Carrier exhibit, Super-Carriers honors all large carriers from the *Forrestal* (CV-59) to the U.S. Navy's most recent super carrier.

Speakers for the dedication included former Chief of Naval Operations, Admiral James L. Holloway III, and the then commanding officer of the *Enterprise*, Captain D.C. Roper. As co-sponsor of the exhibit with Patriots Point, *Enterprise* veterans provided a generous financial donation, artifacts and memorabilia. Large pictures of all super-carriers commissioned through 1992 were and are displayed.

As carrier aircraft became larger, faster and capable of carrying heavier ordnance including nuclear weapons, aircraft carriers were required to accommodate the new planes. The first super-carrier was the *Forrestal*, commissioned in 1955. Three additional members of the class followed: *Saratoga* (CV-60) in 1956; *Ranger* (CV-61) in 1957 and *Independence* (CV-62) in 1959. At the time of this writing, only *Independence* remains in commission.

Four other super-carriers strongly resembling the Forrestal class were built and they too were conventionally powered by oil. The Kitty Hawk class consisted of *Kitty Hawk* CV-63 (commissioned 1961), *Constellation* CV-64 (commissioned 1961) and *America* CV-66 (commissioned 1965). The fourth carrier, *John F. Kennedy* (CV-67), which was commissioned in 1968, was sufficiently different to be classified as a separate class although only a navy professional could tell the difference. Into 1997, only the *Kitty Hawk*, *Constellation* and JFK are still operational. While able to handle all modern jet aircraft, the conventionally powered super-carriers can not compete with the range and endurance of nuclear carriers that can steam for years without refueling.

Although not the first super-carrier, the *Enterprise* was the first nuclear carrier, being commissioned in 1961. Since 1975 all new super-carriers have been nuclear powered beginning with *Nimitz* (CVN-68). Following were *Dwight D. Eisenhower* CVN-69 (commissioned 1977); *Carl Vinson* CVN-70 (1982); *Theodore Roosevelt* CVN-71 (1986); *Abraham Lincoln* CVN-72 (1989); *George Washington* CVN-73 (1992), *John C. Stennis* CVN-74 (1995) and the *Harry S Truman* CVN-75 (1998). Currently under construction is the *Ronald Reagan* CVN-76 (scheduled for 2003).

Many of the super-carriers were active off Vietnam, some served during Desert Storm and all have been available to support foreign policy and quickly project power. Indeed, when crisis or conflict arises, the first question asked in Washington DC is "Where are the carriers?"

While there are variances in exact size and displacement, super-carriers are approximately 1,100 feet long (1,039 for *Forrestal*, 1,123 for *Enterprise*, 1,088 for *Nimitz*), and published figures vary when catapults are included or omitted with displacement ranging from 55,000 tons

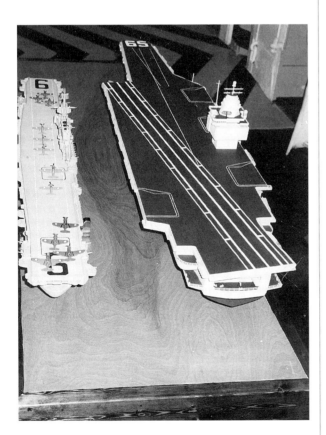

The larger size of the contemporary Enterprise *(CVN-65) is apparent resting beside a same-scale model of the World War II* Enterprise *(CV-6).*

empty to 92,000 when fully loaded. Usual published speed for a nuclear carrier is "about 35 knots," but veterans who served on support vessels during nuclear carrier shakedowns report that their ship was doing 35 knots as the carrier ran away from them. Conventional fueled carriers top speed is approximately 33.5 knots. Aircraft complement, perhaps surprisingly, is similar to World War II era fast carriers that also numbered approximately 90. Most aircraft (all the jet aircraft) displayed on *Yorktown's* flight deck served on super-carriers.

Among items on display in the Super-Carrier exhibit is a builder's plaque from *Enterprise*, a large bronze plaque honoring six officers lost off three carriers (*Saratoga*, *Ranger* and *Theodore Roosevelt*) during the Persian Gulf War, and a 1/16 scale model of *Enterprise* as she appeared when first commissioned (she was significantly modified during a recent overhaul). Immediately beside the nuclear *Enterprise* is a 1/16 scale model of the World War II *Enterprise*. Viewing the two models built to the same scale very quickly educates visitors why the nuclear carriers and their eight oil fueled sisters are termed "Super-Carriers."

"Naval Aviation in the Korean War" Room

THE 'FORGOTTEN WAR' in Korea from 25 June 1950 until the armistice 27 July 1953 cost the United States 54,246 dead, 8,177 missing in action and 389 prisoners of war still unaccounted for. At the time of this writing in 1998, a peace treaty has not been signed.

When the war began, the U.S. Navy had only 10,400 pilots for 9,422 combat aircraft. Only 15 aircraft carriers were in commission. Before the armistice, the Navy had recommissioned another 19 carriers of all types and nearly doubled the number of pilots. During the war, 17 carriers (16 earned battle stars) made 38 deployments to Korea. The carrier air groups contributed significantly to control of the air above Korea. Navy and Marine F9F Panthers and F2H Banshees (both jets), F4U Corsairs and AD Skyraiders fought North Korean and Red Chinese planes, provided close air support, armed reconnaissance and interdiction missions. Further, they attacked ammunition dumps, industrial sites, airfields, railroad yards, bridges, oil refineries and power plants. Nearly 75% of the offensive missions were flown by the World War II era propeller driven Corsairs and Skyraiders. Of the 722 carrier aircraft lost during the war, 358 were attributed to enemy action. Another 532 Navy and Marine aircraft were lost from land and seaplane based units.

One of several photograph/text panels in the "Naval Aviation in the Korean War" Room

Located on the second deck of *Yorktown* in a compartment that earlier served as the Supply Department office, the "Naval Aviation in the Korean War" Room displays numerous photographs of carrier operations and attack missions during the war. Sponsored by Patriots Point, the exhibit features a ten foot model of a long-hull Essex class carrier (most of the Essex class carriers that served off Korea were long-hull), models of a Skyraider, Panther and Corsair (with a four-blade prop characteristic of the Korean era Corsairs), and display cases with artifacts and memorabilia from carriers that earned battle stars during the conflict. Most artifacts are from the *Leyte* (CV-32) including several compartment designators, a gyro repeater compass, voice tube cover, 20mm gun canister and an infrared viewing set. A flight jacket and pilot's helmet from the *Philippine Sea* (CV-47) plus paper items from *Boxer* (CV-21) and *Valley Forge* (CV-45) are displayed in separate cases. A large panel courtesy of the Tailhook Association provides a detailed overview of naval aviation in the Korean War, and another presents a photographic record of the dangers of carrier deck operations. The deck operations panel presents pictures of a Corsair jumping the crash barrier,

then striking two parked planes before flying off Princeton's portside. Helicopters first proved their value in Korea, and should another conflict precede a peace treaty in the region, helicopters may play an even greater role.

Korean War Aircraft Carrier Battle Star Totals

USS PHILIPPINE SEA CV-47	9
USS VALLEY FORGE CV-45	8
USS PRINCETON CV-37	8
USS BOXER CV-21	8
USS BATAAN CVL-29	7
USS BADOENG STRAIT CVE-116	6
USS SICILY CVE-118	5
USS BON HOMME RICHARD CV-31	5
USS ESSEX CV-9	4
USS BAIROKO CVE-115	3
USS LEYTE CV-32	2
USS KEARSARGE CV-33	2
USS ORISKANY CV-34	2
USS ANTIETAM CV-36	2
USS RENDOVA CVE-114	2
USS LAKE CHAMPLAIN CV-39	1

6

Remembrance of The Surface Navy

World War II Battleship Exhibit

WHAT IS BELIEVED TO BE the most comprehensive exhibit to honor World War II battleships was dedicated at Patriots Point 7 December 1991, the 50th anniversary of the attack on Pearl Harbor. All 25 battleships that received one or more battle stars in World War II are honored in the large exhibit on the second deck aboard *Yorktown* in a compartment which once served as a barber shop and later as ship's store. Sponsored by Patriots Point, the exhibit dedication and Pearl Harbor observance was attended by over 3,000 people including several hundred veterans of the battleship *Washington* (BB-56).

The battleship reigned supreme in the minds of many naval leaders in the major countries engaged in the global conflict of 1939–1945. Although the naval aspect of the war proved to be essentially a carrier and submarine war, the battleship nonetheless affected thinking and strategy from the beginning to near the end. For both the United States and Japan, battleships were used with some hesitancy. At the critical juncture of the battle for Guadalcanal (November 1942), the Japanese committed two battleships. Both were sunk in those confined waters, and it was not until the U.S. Navy arrived off the Philippines in late 1944 and Okinawa in 1945 that Japan finally committed its total battleship strength to combat. Only once did an American battleship sink a Japanese battleship (*Washington* sank *Kirishima* off Guadalcanal), but six

*World War II
Battleship Room.*

old battleships helped sink two already wounded Japanese battleships in the 25 October 1944 Surigao Strait engagement during the Battle of Leyte Gulf. In the Atlantic theater, *Massachusetts* (BB-59) silenced the docked Vichy French battleship *Jean Bart* in November 1942.

While the anticipated decisive battleline action never occurred, U.S. Navy battleships were particularly successful in the relatively unanticipated roles as bombardment and anti-aircraft platforms. Although not as glamorous as dueling with enemy battleships, bombardment and anti-aircraft duties were nonetheless dangerous. Shore bombardment tied the ships to a small area exposing them to shore batteries, submarines and air attacks. *Colorado* (BB-45) was hit 22 times off Tinian.

All four Iowa class battleships served during the Korean War. *New Jersey* (BB-62) was activated for service off Vietnam: *Missouri* (BB-63) and *Wisconsin* (BB-64) participated in the Persian Gulf War.

The Patriots Point WWII Battleship Exhibit had its origins in a December 1989 Pearl Harbor display. That display, which included a large diorama of Pearl Harbor as it appeared on 7 December 1941, was incorporated into the permanent exhibit. Particularly noteworthy in the permanent exhibit is a series of seven to ten toot models representing several of the respective battleship classes. Included is a six and a half foot model of *Arizona* (BB-39), built by Charleston resident William Blackmore; a ten foot model of the *Iowa*; seven foot models of the *South Dakota* (BB-57), *Tennessee* (BB-43); and an eight foot model of the *Washington*. Summersville resident Terry Mosley crafted the *South Dakota*, *Tennessee* and *Washington*.

Major artifacts include a piece of watertight bulkhead from the aft turret of the sunken *Arizona*; a telephone directory from the *Nevada* (BB-36) still showing the effects of being underwater; gunnery plaques removed from the *West Virginia* (BB-48); tickets and the sword of a commanding officer from the *Oklahoma* (BB-37); and some decking from the *New Jersey*. (*Nevada*, *Oklahoma* and *West Virginia* were also sunk at Pearl Harbor as well as the *California*.) On display from the *Washington* is a steering wheel and piece of decking.

Battleships Lost in World War II

USS OKLAHOMA BB-37
USS ARIZONA BB-39

World War II Battleships by Class with Battle Star Totals

Iowa Class
IOWA BB-61 (9); NEW JERSEY BB-62 (9); MISSOURI BB-63 (3); WISCONSIN BB-64 (5)

South Dakota Class
South Dakota BB-57 (13); Indiana BB-58 (9); Massachusetts BB-59 (11); Alabama BB-60 (9)

North Carolina Class
North Carolina BB-55 (15); Washington BB-56 (13)

Colorado Class
Colorado BB-45 (7); Maryland BB-46 (7); West Virginia BB-48 (5)

Tennessee Class
TENNESSE BB-43 (10); CALIFORNIA BB-44 (7)

New Mexico Class
NEW MEXICO BB-40 (6); MISSISSIPPI BB-41 (8); IDAHO BB-42 (7)

Pennsylvania Class
PENNSYLVANIA BB-38 (8); ARIZONA BB-39 (1)

Nevada Class
NEVADA BB-36 (7); OKLAHOMA BB-37 (1)

New York Class
NEW YORK BB-34 (3); TEXAS BB-35 (5)

USS Missouri BB-63 Room

OTHER THAN the *Arizona*, probably no other battleship's name is more recognized than that of the *Missouri* (BB-63). "Big Mo" won only three battle stars during World War II, but she carried the name of the home state of President Harry S Truman. That, plus the fact that the *Missouri* was a flagship for the victorious U.S. Navy as it prepared to enter Tokyo, led to the decision for the 2 September 1945 formal surrender of the Japanese to be held on the main deck of the Iowa class battleship.

Commissioned 11 June 1944, *Missouri* did not see action until 1945. Her nine 16 inch guns and 20 five inch guns shelled Iwo Jima, Okinawa and the Japanese home islands in the last months of the war. During the Korean War the battleship was awarded five battle stars for bombardment duty. Decommissioned 26 February 1955, the ship rested in the mothball fleet at Bremerton, Washington, until commissioned again 10 May 1986. In her final configuration the battleship retained her nine 16 inch guns and 12 five inch guns. Added were Tomahawk and Harpoon cruise missiles and four Phalanx close-in-weapons. Cruise missiles were fired by the ship during the Persian Gulf War.

Located on the fourth deck of *Yorktown*, the Missouri Room was dedicated by veterans of the ship and Patriots Point staff on 3 September 1989. Present for the occasion was 91 year old former commanding officer, Rear Admiral William F. Callaghan. Included in the exhibit room are pieces of a Japanese suicide plane that struck the ship 11 April 1945, a surrender plaque cast from the mold of the original plaque, a 54 inch model of the ship as configured in 1945, and a replica of the surrender table with many pictures depicting the surrender ceremony.

World War II Cruiser Exhibit

ON THE 51ST ANNIVERSARY of the attack on Pearl Harbor, Patriots Point Naval & Maritime Museum opened a new exhibit honoring the 74 heavy and light cruisers that won battle stars during World War II. Representatives of cruiser veterans groups attended the 7 December 1992 ceremony aboard *Yorktown*. The Patriots Point exhibit was—and yet may be—unique in American naval museums as no other comprehensive World War II cruiser exhibit existed at that time. No cruiser engaged in battle during World War II was preserved in museum status, all having been scrapped or sunk.

The World War II Cruiser Exhibit is permanently located on the *Yorktown's* second deck and spans three compartments. Nine models ranging from three to seven feet in length honor respective cruiser classes. Display panels honoring each cruiser class are arranged throughout the exhibit while artifacts and memorabilia are displayed throughout.

Two of the most unique artifacts to be found

Missouri *(BB-63) Room*

Ten-foot Iowa class model

Unique artifacts abound in the World War II American Cruiser Exhibit.

Five-foot model of Arizona (BB-39)

Portion of World War II American Cruiser Exhibit.

anywhere in the museum are located in this exhibit. First is the only surviving piece of the *Indianapolis* (CA-35), the last major warship lost by the U.S. Navy in World War II. Under repair from a kamikaze hit in the summer of 1945, a fast ship was urgently needed to carry major components of the atom bomb which would be dropped on Hiroshima. In the haste to sail, CA-35's builders plaque was not reinstalled on the vessel. When the ship was sunk by a Japanese submarine on the return voyage, the historical value of the plaque was immediately recognized and it was forwarded to the Washington Navy Yard. In 1960 the Curator of the Navy reported the plaque missing from inventory as it was inadvertently mislabeled. Transferred to Patriots Point carrying a manifest label as being the builders plaque of the *Biloxi* (CL-80), the error was discovered and the Curator of the Navy generously allowed Patriots Point to continue display of the historic artifact.

The second unique artifact is a porthole from the *Houston* (CV-30). While portholes are fairly common as display items, few, if any, have "re-turned from the dead."

Fighting against overwhelming odds, *Houston* went down in the early hours of 1 March 1942. Many years later, divers found the ship in relatively shallow water in Sunda Strait near Australia and they cut the porthole from the ship. Donated to the government of Australia, that country returned it to the United States and to the veterans association of the valiant ship (fewer than 300 survived the battle, the sinking and three years as prisoners of war in Japan). After considering other offers, the *Houston* veterans elected to donate the sacred artifact to Patriots Point for permanent display in the World War II Cruiser Exhibit.

Among the other significant artifacts in this exhibit are a bell removed from the *Northampton* (CV-26) just before she was lost in action in 1942; a builders plaque from the *Mobile* (CL-63); a piece of the German guided bomb that killed over 200 on the *Savannah* (CL-42); a porthole from the *Portland* (CA-33); and several steering and valve wheels from *Canberra* (CA-70), *Houston* (CL-81), *St. Paul* (CA-73) and

Columbia CL-56 (CL-56 was named for South Carolina's state capital).

Seven heavy cruisers and three light cruisers were lost in action during World War II. Seven were lost in the dark days of 1942 when cruisers were thrust into the void resulting from the loss and damage to battleships at Pearl Harbor on 7 December 1941. Not lost during World War II was the *Phoenix* (CL-46), which was in Pearl Harbor on the "day of infamy," but she was sunk by a British submarine during the 1982 Falklands War having been transferred to Argentina.

Seven-foot Farragut *(DD-348) model aboard* Laffey.

Cruisers Lost in World War II

ATLANTA CL-51
ASTORIA CA-34
CHICAGO CV-29
HELENA CL-50
HOUSTON CA-30
INDIANAPOLIS CA-35
JUNEAU CL-52
NORTHAMPTON CA-26
QUINCY CA-39
VINCENNES CA-44

Battle Star Leaders

SAN FRANCISCO CA-38   17
MINNEAPOLIS CA-36   17
NEW ORLEANS CA-32   17
PORTLAND CA-33   16
SAN DIEGO CL-53   15

World War II Destroyer Memorial Exhibit

THE ONLY KNOWN comprehensive memorial exhibit honoring the hundreds of U.S. Navy destroyers that fought in World War II was dedicated 14 April 1989 on the main deck of the *Laffey* (DD-724). Among those speaking during the ceremony was Rear Admiral Julian Becton, USN(Ret) who was the commanding officer of the *Laffey* when she was struck by kamikazes in 1945. On the evening before the main ceremony, a torch lighting service honored the 88 destroyers lost during World War II.

Over 350 destroyers were built during the war to serve with 173 already in commission when the war began. An additional 46 "flush-deckers" were in commission as fast minelayers (8 DM), fast minesweepers (18 DMS), high-speed transports (4 APD), seaplane tenders (14 AVD) and other auxiliary types (2).

The first of the post-World War I destroyers were members of the Farragut class. These ships, completed in 1934–35, were the first destroyers to emphasize anti-aircraft protection, and main armament was the 5-inch gun instead of the 3-inch or 4-inch guns of the flush-deckers. After the Farraguts came the Mahans and the Porters (completed 1936–37), the Somers and Gridleys (1937–38), the Benhams and Sims (1939–40), the Bensons—including the Gleaves, Livermores and Bristols (1940–43), the Fletchers (1942–44), the Allen M. Sumners (1943–45), and finally, the Gearings (1944–46).

Construction of the World War II Destroyer Memorial Exhibit required over 2,500 man hours. Two large compartments, used to accommodate officers serving aboard *Laffey* when she was in commission, were completely gutted to provide space for the new exhibit. The forward compartment is designed to describe in pictures and engraved text-plates the many functions of World War II destroyers including surface actions, shore gunfire support, convoy escort, submarine hunter, anti-aircraft platform, plane guard, rescue vessel, fast transport and mine warfare.

The aft compartment is an "Honors Room" featuring Presidential Unit Citation and Navy Unit Commendation recipients, battle star leaders and the 88 World War II destroyers lost to combat action, storms and accidents. All lost destroyers are listed with a special plaque honoring the three destroyers lost with all hands (*Pillsbury* DD-227, *Edsall* DD-219 and *Jarvis* DD-393).

Throughout the exhibit original artwork complements prints of World War II destroyers in action. Among the destroyer models on display is a seven foot replica of the *Farragut* (DD-348), commissioned in 1934 and remembered as the first modern destroyer to be built after the first World War. Other models honor the highly successful wartime-built Fletcher class destroyers and the older World War I era flush-deck four stack destroyers.

Among artifacts and memorabilia currently displayed are a flag from the *Hammann* (DD-412), a one-time Charleston-based destroyer sunk alongside the first carrier *Yorktown* at the Battle of Midway; a match cover from the *Hobson* (DD-464), a Charleston-built destroyer that compiled a distinguished World War II record before being run over by an aircraft carrier in 1952; and the last letter sent home by a sailor lost in the infamous December 1944 typhoon which cost the U.S. Navy three destroyers.

As both World War II destroyers named *Laffey* won the Presidential Unit Citation and the first (DD-459) was lost in action, each is included but not highlighted in this exhibit. Despite the exhibit's emphasis on destroyers in general, the significant history of the surviving *Laffey* is recalled by an engraved plaque noting that on 16 April 1945 thirty-two officers and men died and 71 were wounded within and adjacent to the two compartments now housing the World War II Destroyer Memorial.

Destroyers Lost in World War II

Aaron Ward DD-483
Abner Read DD-526
Barry DD-248, APD-29
Barton DD-599
Beatty DD-640
Benham DD-397
Blue DD-387
Borie DD-215
Bristol DD-453
Brownson DD-518
Buck DD-420
Bush DD-529
Callaghan DD-792
Chevalier DD-451
Calhoun DD-801
Colhoun DD-85, APD-2
Cooper DD-695
Corry DD-463
Cushing DD-376
DeHaven DD-469
Dickerson DD-157, APD-21
Drexler DD-741
Duncan DD-485
Edsall DD-219
Emmons DD-457
Gamble DD-123
Glennon DD-620
Gregory DD-82, APD-3
Gwin DD-433
Halligan DD-584
Hammann DD-412
Henley DD-391

HOEL DD-533
HOVEY DD-208, DMS-11
HULL DD-350
INGRAHAM DD-444
JOCOB JONES DD-130
JARVIS DD-393
JOHNSTON DD-557
LAFFEY DD-459
LANDSDALE DD-426
LEARY DD-158
LITTLE DD-79, APD-4
LITTLE DD-803
LONG DD-209, DMS-12
LONGSHAW DD-559
LUCE DD-552
MADDOX DD-622
MAHAN DD-364
MANNERI L. ABELE DD-733
MCKEAN DD-90, APD-5
MEREDITH DD-434
MEREDITH DD-726
MONAGHAN DD-354
MONSSEN DD-436
MONTGOMERY DD-121, DM-17
MORRISON DD-560
NOA DD-343, APD-24
O'BRIEN DD-415
PALMER DD-161, DMS-5
PARROTT DD-218
PEARY DD-226
PERKINS DD-377
PERRY DD-340, DMS-17
PILSBURY DD-227
POPE DD-225
PORTER DD-356
PRESTON DD-379
PRINGLE DD-477
REID DD-369
REUBEN JAMES DD-245
ROWAN DD-405
SIMS DD-409
SPENCE DD-512
STEWART DD-224
STRONG DD-467
STURTEVANI DD-DD-240
THORTON DD-270, AVD-11
TRUXIUN DD-229

TUCKER DD-374
TURNER DD-648
TWIGGS DD-591
WALKE DD-DD-416
WARD DD-139, APD-16
WARRINGTON DD-383
WASMUTH DD-338, DMS-15
WILLIAM D. PORTER, DD-579
WORDEN DD-352

Battle Star Leaders

O'BANNON DD-450	17
MAURY DD-401	16
RUSSELL DD-414	16
SAUFLEY DD-465	16
NICHOLAS DD-449	16
MORRIS DD-417	15
BUCHANAN DD-484	15
TAYLOR DD-468	15
FLETCHER DD-445	15
FARRAGUT DD-348	14
CONYNHAM DD-371	14
HUGHES DD-410	14
EDWARDS DD-619	14
JENKINS DD-447	14

Destroyer Escort Exhibit

MOST OF THE 498 destroyer escorts built during World War II served with the U.S. Navy. Great Britain received most of the 92 destroyer escorts that were transferred, or leased, to Allied powers with Brazil and France receiving the others. Like their larger "big sister" destroyers (DD), some destroyer escorts (DE) were also converted to fast transports. In terms of overall characteristics as compared to destroyers, destroyer escorts were lighter in standard displacement (1,400 tons), shorter (306 feet), carried a smaller complement (approximately 210), and slower (23–24 knots). However, the mass-produced destroyer escort was more maneuverable and less expensive than a destroyer. The attribute of maneuverability was particularly favorable as the primary function of

Samuel B. Roberts (DE-413), lost during the Battle off Samar, 25 October 1944

Portion of Destroyer Escort Exhibit aboard Laffey

the destroyer escort was to track, pursue and attack submarines. Although the destroyer escort did not carry armament to greatly challenge surface vessels (main armament was either two 5-inch guns or three three-inch), they did carry a full complement of anti-submarine weapons (usually two depth charge tracks, eight single DC projectors and one multiple projector). Toward the end of the war, some destroyer escorts lost their single 21-inch, triple torpedo tubes in favor of more anti-aircraft guns. Typical original anti-aircraft weaponry consisted of one 40mm twin, four 40mm singles and ten 20mm.

In their role as part of the carrier-destroyer-destroyer escort "hunter-killer" team, the destroyer escorts' contribution cannot be overstated. These teams proved to be the weapon that enemy submarines could not defeat, and the formerly offense-minded submarine became prey instead of pursuer from early 1943 to war's end. Although smaller and slower, several destroyer escorts established war records as memorable as any battleship, carrier, cruiser, destroyer or submarine. Among the best remembered destroyer escorts are *England* (DE-635) which killed six Japanese submarines in less than two weeks; *John C. Butler* DE-339 (five battle stars, Presidential Unit Citation, Navy Unit Commendation and survivor of "Taffy 3" in the Battle off Samar); *Bronstein* DE-189 (four battle stars, Presidential Unit Citation and primarily responsible for the sinking of three U-boats); and *Lawrence C. Taylor* DE-415 (seven battle stars and credited with sinking two Japanese submarines including I-26 which sank the U.S. Navy cruiser *Juneau* CL-52 in November 1942).

The Destroyer Escort Exhibit is located aboard *Laffey* in the former helicopter hangar. Placed in 1986 and sponsored by Patriots Point and veterans of destroyer escorts, the exhibit offers a generous display of memorabilia. Included are multiple art prints and photographs, three 30-inch models, flags, kamikaze pieces, uniforms, battle helmets and the medals (including Navy Cross) awarded Ensign John C. Butler. Among the artifacts displayed are the steering stand and wheel from the *Merrill* (DE-392), and the commissioning ensign and pennant for the *Abercrombie* (DE-343). Nearly a dozen builder's plaques are displayed.

Destroyer Escorts Lost in World War II

BATES DE-68, APD-47 (1945)
EVERSOLE DE-404 (1944)
FECHTELER DE-157 (1944)
FISKE DE-143 (1944)
FREDERICK C. DAVIS DE-136 (1945)
HOLDER DE-401 (1944)
LEOPOLD DE-319 (1944)
OBERRENDER DE-344 (1945)
RICH DE-695 (1944)
SAMUEL B. ROBERTS DE-413 (1944)
SHELTON DE-407 (1944)
UNDERHILL DE-682 (1945)

Destroyer Escort Battle Star Leaders

RIDDLE DE-185	12
BANGUST DE-739	11
ENGLAND DE-635	10
SWEARER DE-186	9
LAMONS DE-743	9
MITCHELL DE-43	9
WEAVER DE-741	9
WATERMAN DE-740	8
REYNOLDS DE-42	8
HILBERT DE-742	8
SAMUEL S. MILES DE-183	8

Charleston Naval Shipyard Exhibit

ONE OF THE FIRST exhibits to be placed after the *Yorktown* opened to the public was the Charleston Naval Shipyard Exhibit. Located in passageways port and starboard of the number one elevator, the exhibit was expanded and upgraded in late 1995 and early 1996 just before the 15 March 1996 closing of the shipyard and Naval Base.

The waterfront land upon which the Naval Base and shipyard were built was formerly used as a rice plantation and recreational area (Chicora Park). Acquired by the Navy in 1901, construction began in 1902, shops and dry-dock number one were in place by 1909. In 1913 the yard built the first of the 253 vessels to be constructed by the facility. During World War I employment rose to over 1,700 and the first warship, the gunboat *Asheville*, was built. After the war, the yard concentrated on maintenance of mine sweepers and gunboats until 1933 when the facility was upgraded to a new construction shipyard. Coast Guard cutters, tug boats and destroyers were built during the Depression era and the yard was a proven entity as World War II began in Europe in September 1939.

Employment rose from about 2,400 in 1939 to 9,000 in 1941 when the United States entered World War II, making the shipyard the largest industrial employer in South Carolina's history. By 1943 nearly 26,000 were employed (including 5,000 women) to build, repair and maintain ships actively participating in the war. Three new dry-docks were built and the expanded shipyard constructed 216 vessels during the war including 20 destroyers, 17 destroyer escorts, 9 fast troop transports, 92 medium landing ships and one de-

Views of the Charleston Naval Shipyard Exhibit

stroyer tender. Twelve vessels built by the shipyard were lost during the war including 5 destroyers.

Shortly after World War II, onset of the Cold War dictated new roles for the shipyard. Instead of decommissioning and preserving warships, the yard emphasized repair, overhaul and conversion of ships including submarines beginning in 1948. By 1959 the yard prepared to begin refueling and overhauls for nuclear submarines. Despite being successful in all its tasks, the shipyard and the Charleston Naval Base, by the late 1980's the third largest naval base in the United States behind Norfolk and San Diego, became casualties as the Cold War ended.

Before moving to other jobs and other areas, 36 employees of the Charleston Naval Shipyard joined with Patriots Point staff to gather artifacts and memorabilia from the yard, and to contribute to the expansion and remodeling of the exhibit aboard *Yorktown*. The exhibit covers the early history of the yard along with World War I, World War II, and the Cold War era. Photographs and text provide visitors with a historical background while numerous artifacts and models document the work of thousands of civilians and Navy personnel from 1901 into 1996. Several of the destroyer and submarine models are over 10 feet in length: smaller models, especially those resting in models of the dry-docks, capture a realistic ambiance. Personalizing the exhibit are the pictures and listings of former commandants and commanding officers of the facility, and a compartment arranged as an office honoring the late L. Mendel Rivers. Congressman Rivers served 35 years in the House of Representatives and for the 89th, 90th and 91st Congresses he was Chairman of the House Armed Services, and was noted for his strong advocacy of nuclear propulsion.

Particularly interesting to many visitors are the artifacts from the shipyard dating back to 1916. Early typewriters, telephones, office equipment, and an old electric shop panel are displayed along with diving suits, a pipe shop display, welders shop exhibit, paint shop display and a compartment populated with manikins in yard working clothes. One of many small canteen buildings is centered in the large exhibit area.

Among the wartime artifacts on display is a flag flown by the Charleston-built destroyer *Sterett* (DD-407) during the momentous Naval Battle of Guadalcanal in November 1942; and a display honoring the Charleston-built destroyer *Hobson* (DD-464, DMS-26). Awarded the Presidential Unit Citation for World War II action, the destroyer was rammed and sunk by the carrier *Wasp* 26 April 1952.

All five of the U.S. Navy ships named *Charleston* are remembered with pictures and text-plates, the 1905 bell for the World War I era cruiser and a six foot model of the 1888 launched protected cruiser. Rosters are mounted throughout the exhibit in honor of the ships built in Charleston while several ship banners draw memories back to their time in the shipyard.

A large area of the exhibit is devoted to the era when POMFLANT was active in the Charleston area. The Polaris Missile Facility Atlantic display offers models, photos and text to educate visitors to one of the many significant roles in the eventful history of the Charleston Naval facilities.

Amphibious Forces Exhibit

OPENED IN 1997, the Amphibious Forces Exhibit honors the landing craft and forces that carried Allied forces across the Pacific, Atlantic and Mediterranean in World War II and landed them on numerous beachheads. In December 1941 no LSTs (Landing Ship Tank) were in commission, but concept designs were being developed. Strategic planning for both the Atlantic and Pacific was forged, in part, around the development and availability of LSTs and other landing craft.

LSTs displaced up to 1650 tons, were 327 feet in length and carried a crew of up to 120. Despite a beam of only 50 feet, an LST could carry tanks, vehicles, cargo and ordnance. Designed to carry equipment onto a beach, the bow opened to lower a ramp for expeditious exiting of cargo. Just over 1,000 LSTs were built during World War II and some were used during the

Korean War. More a reflection of contemporary warfare than a matter of budget, there are only two LSTs in current inventory.

Derivations of the LST were the LSM (Landing Ship Medium), a smaller vessel of some 490 tons measuring 203×34 feet; the LCI (Landing Craft Infantry), an even smaller craft—159× 23 feet—that operated between beachheads and larger transports off shore and could carry 200 troops plus cargo; the LCT (Landing Craft Tank) 119×32 feet; and LCS (Landing Craft Support) which measured 157×23 feet. As the war progressed, these vessels carried armament ranging from 20 mm and 40 mm anti-aircraft guns to rockets.

The Patriots Point exhibit offers text, photographs and models of various landing craft. Currently, the exhibit is located on the third deck of *Yorktown*.

U.S. *Naval Advanced Tactical Support Base, South Vietnam*

UNIQUE AMONG MUSEUMS is the U.S. Naval Advanced Tactical Support Base (ATSB), "Somewhere," South Vietnam, located land-side at Patriots Point Museum. A large scale reconstruction, the Support Base offers visitors a realistic combat environment that existed along the inland waterways of South Vietnam beginning in 1965. Twenty such lightly fortified bases, manned by six officers and 59 enlisted men, were established to help obtain control of the inland and coastal waters of South Vietnam. Inland control, especially in the Mekong Delta, was particularly difficult as these bases usually attempted to maintain patrols and surveillance for only a 35 mile radius while some 3,000 miles of waterways existed in the country.

A Support Base provided repair, maintenance, supply storage, quartering and messing facilities for crews of 10 PBRs (River Patrol Boat), and had either landing pads or mobile afloat barges for UH-1 helicopters. To help keep sea lanes open to Saigon, to board and inspect, intercept gun runners and supplies to the Viet

Cong, especially from Cambodia, and even conduct psychological operations, the PBRs usually operated in teams of two and covered each other at ranges from 300 to 600 yards.

Appropriately, the first display upon entering the Patriots Point exhibit that was dedicated 20 February 1993 is a Mark I PBR. Authorization for 250 of the 31 foot fiberglass boats with a draft of only 10 inches was authorized by 1968. Powered by two General Motors 6V53 diesel engines coupled to Jacuzzi jet pumps and capable of speeds up to 35 knots in the Mark II, the PBR carried a crew of four (boat captain, engineer, gunner and seaman). Normal armament consisted of two .50 caliber machine guns forward, two M-60 machine guns port and starboard, one .50 aft and a Mark 18 grenade launcher. Successful with and without helicopter support, the PBR has special significance for two former "Brown Water sailors" instrumental in the placement of the exhibit. Former Patriots Point Development Authority Board of Directors member, James Elliott Williams, was awarded the Congressional Medal of Honor for leading his two PBRs against a much larger force and destroying 65 enemy boats on 31 October 1965. And the exhibit's designer, E.G. "Buddy" Sturgis, was wounded while serving on a PBR 16 July 1969.

The buildings within the exhibit were constructed by U.S. Navy Seabees. Along with the two Huey helicopters and jeeps, a visitor will observe a base perimeter constructed of empty 55 gallon fuel drums, barrier wire and fill dirt, concertina wire at the top of fencing and a 24-foot observation/gun tower, the interior of which doubles as a shower. In the hot, humid environment of South Vietnam, pallets used to transport ammunition, food and other supplies, were welcome for use as walkways around the base during the monsoon season. An ammunition bunker, a combat information center (CIC) with the sounds of radio transmissions, a small generator station, latrine, Sick Bay, supply store, living area, chow hall and mortar pit replicate installations common to all support bases. Connex containers offer artifacts and memorabilia from veterans who were part of the Brown Water Navy.

One connex box is dedicated to General William C. Westmoreland, a Charleston resident who served as Commander, U.S. Military Assistance Command, Vietnam. Near the General Westmoreland display is another containing a large collection of weapons used during the Vietnam War. This display offers both United States and communist weapons, some used earlier by the French, Germans, Soviets and Chinese.

In appreciation to the Navy Seabee Unit 412 that built the sea huts, the mess hall is dedicated to the memory of Congressional Medal of Honor recipient Construction Mechanic Third Class Marvin Glen Shields. Shields' heroic actions cost his life in June 1965 while serving with the Seabees in South Vietnam.

Views of the U.S. Naval Advanced Tactical Support Base, "Somewhere," South Vietnam

7

Thematic Exhibits

Black Americans Military Exhibit

O N 13 JANUARY 1997 seven black Americans were awarded the Congressional Medal of Honor for their heroic actions during World War II. The awards not only recognized these men some 50 plus years after they performed their deeds, but also called to attention a general oversight of the major contributions of black Americans in this country's military history.

One of the first to die during the American Revolution was a black man, Crispus Attucks. During the Civil War 220,000 blacks served in the Union Army and 37,500 died. The Confederacy was sustained during the war by blacks serving in a host of logistical roles such as building fortifications and digging trenches in addition to sustaining the food supply. Over 430,000 blacks served in World War I and over a million served during World War II. In 1948, legislation integrated blacks into the armed forces in place of the previous practice of having all-black units. Before integration, numerous black units served with distinction, perhaps the best known being the 54th Massachusetts Infantry of Civil War fame and the 332nd Fighter Group, 99th Pursuit Squadron ("the Tuskegee Airmen") of World War II fame.

The Patriots Point exhibit honoring blacks in the military alternates between the second deck compartment which last served as the ship's chapel and the hangar deck. Each February, in honor of Black History Month, the exhibit is

Views within the Black Americans Military Exhibit

Black sailors man 20mm anti-aircraft guns aboard an aircraft carrier during World War II. USN

moved to the hangar deck. The exhibit offers paintings depicting black military themes such as the "Buffalo Soldiers" and 54th Massachusetts Infantry assault on Fort Wagner (a Confederate fort only a few miles south of the *Yorktown*, but now under water). The builder's plaque for the USS *Jesse L. Brown* is displayed in memory of Lt.j.g. Brown who died on 4 December 1950 while flying close combat support for Marines near Chosen Reservoir, Korea. Photographs are mounted in honor of General Colin L. Powell, the first black to become Chairman of the Joint Chiefs of Staff; General Benjamin O. Davis, Sr., the first black general in the United States military service (an Army general, his son became with the same name became the first black general in the U.S. Air Force); General Daniel "Chappie" James, the first black four star general (U.S. Air Force); Brigadier General Hazel Winifred Johnson, the first black female general (U.S. Army); and Vice Admiral Samuel L. Gravely, Jr., the first black admiral in the United States Navy.

Women in the U.S. Military Exhibit

WOMEN HAVE BEEN PART of America's military since the American Revolution. Through much of the 19th century, their roles were tertiary for the most part. By the Civil War women were under contract as nurses, and in 1901 the Army Nurse Corps was established although no rank was awarded. The Navy followed suit in 1908. Personnel demands for clerical work during World War I led to women being enlisted in several services (notably not the Army), but the practice ceased with the end of the war in 1918. Soon after the beginning of World War II, however, women were sought in large numbers for a variety of occupations within the military structure in order to free men for combat operations. The Women's Army Auxiliary Corps (WAACs/ WACs) was established 14 May 1942, and by the end of the war in 1945 nearly 100,000 women had served. The Navy accepted over 86,000 women beginning 30 June 1942 in the Women Accepted for Voluntary Emergency Service (WAVES) program. The Coast Guard after 23 November 1942 accepted over 10,000 for its reserve (SPARS), and the Women's Reserve of the U.S. Marine Corps was developed on 13 February 1943 with over 18,000 women serving. During World War II 57,000 women served in the Army Nursing Corps while over 11,000 served in the Navy Nursing Corps.

During World War II women proved to be competent through a wide range of military occupations, even proving themselves as non-combat pilots. The value of women in the U.S. military was officially recognized in 1948 when the Women's Armed Services Act included women in the permanent military structure. Growth was slow, even during the Korean War, but outstanding service in Vietnam and the end of the draft in the 1970s expanded opportunities for women in the military services. Beginning in 1976 women were admitted to the military academies, and the service of 41,000 women in the combat theater during the Persian Gulf War ended much debate concerning the capability of women to serve. The extent of combat duty for women is still being debated, but their value to the military is not an issue. In 1997 women comprised 14 percent of the United States military.

The Women in the U.S. Military Exhibit was dedicated on 11 November 1993. Sponsored by State Senator Arthur Ravenel, Jr., and Representative Harry M. Hallman, Jr., the exhibit is currently located on the second deck of *Yorktown* near the former location of the ship's chapel. With the active support of Isle of Palms Mayor Carmen Bunch, a veteran of World War II, the exhibit offers uniforms representing all services with various ranks, recruiting posters and numerous period photographs. Particularly noteworthy is a uniform donated by Rear Admiral Veronica Zasdni Froman, only the 16th female naval officer selected for flag rank, and a former com-

manding officer (1993) of the Naval Station, Charleston, South Carolina.

Maritime Legends

THE MARITIME LEGENDS EXHIBIT at Patriots Point is a work in progress. Initially planned for display aboard NS *Savannah*—the world's first nuclear merchant ship—when she was a member of the Patriots Point Museum Fleet (1981-1994), the display is currently aboard *Yorktown*. To date, displays have been placed for RMS *Titanic*, RMS *Lusitania*, RMS *Queen Mary*, RMS *Queen Elizabeth* and *Normandie*. Artifacts are being collected for other ships including *Andrea Doria* and the *United States*.

As a work in progress, "maritime legends" is loosely defined as the availability of artifacts and art prints will help determine future expansion. A common denominator is "disaster." Five of the six ships had sad endings and the one remaining, *Queen Mary*, has encountered challenges to her survival as a hotel/museum.

RMS *Titanic* (RMS=Royal Mail Ship) may be the best known maritime legend. The largest (46,000 tons and 882 feet long) and most luxurious liner of its day, *Titanic* was steaming near

Uniforms are featured in the Women in the U.S. Military Exhibit

her top speed of 22 knots when she struck an iceberg south of Newfoundland shortly before midnight 14 April 1912. Three hours later, at 2:20 am on 15 April, the White Star liner sank with a loss of 1,513, over two-thirds of those aboard. The disaster prompted the International Convention for Safety at Sea in 1913 to require ships to have lifeboats for all passengers, and a 24 hour radio watch. Further, an international Ice Patrol was formed. The Patriots Point exhibit offers a 56 inch model of *Titanic* (note the White Star Line yellow painted funnels), art prints of the sinking and underwater views, and period post cards featuring the legendary liner.

RMS *Lusitania* began Atlantic service in 1907, and succumbed to German U-boat *(U-20)* torpedoes on 7 May 1915 just off the coast of Ireland. Capable of carrying 2,150 passengers,

over 1,200 went down in 18 minutes with the 785 foot Cunard liner. *Lusitania* (41,440 displacement) had a top speed of 26 knots, well above the nine knot speed of a German submarine, but the U-boat torpedoes had a speed of 40 knots. The sinking contributed to anti-German public opinion in the United States, which entered the war on 2 April 1917 three months after Germany opted for unrestricted submarine warfare. The Patriots Point exhibit offers a 48 inch model of *Lusitania* with art prints, books written about the ship and period post cards. A visitor will note the red painted funnels characteristic of Cunard Line vessels.

RMS *Queen Mary* and RMS *Queen Elizabeth* were also Cunard Line ships. Intended to restore Great Britain to supremacy in Atlantic liner service, the two great Queens would have

Lafayette (AP-53) just after burning and capsizing at New York in February 1942. Formerly the French line Normandie, the ship was seized after Germany declared war on the United States in December 1941

Four to five-foot models are displayed in the Maritime Legends Exhibit.
Shown here from front to back are Lusitania, Titanic *and* Queen Mary

accomplished their mission except for the interruption of World War II. *Queen Mary* made her maiden voyage 27 May 1936 and was indeed the Queen of the Seas until forced into wartime duty as a troopship. At 1,019 feet and 81,000 tons, the liner could carry 2,030 passengers in luxury, or over 15,000 troops in comfort if not luxury. With an average speed of 28.5 knots, the liner—painted gray and nicknamed "Gray Ghost" during the war, was allowed to steam alone on her many wartime voyages. Although never attacked by U-boats, disaster visited *Queen Mary* on 2 October 1942 when the British light cruiser HMS *Curacao* turned in front of the troopship. The collision sank the cruiser with 338 of 439 crew lost. Returned to passenger service in July 1947, *Queen Mary* carried passengers between Europe and the United States into 1967. Converted to a floating hotel and museum in 1971, she continues life in San Diego. The Patriots Point exhibit offers a 64 inch model of *Queen Mary* with art prints, dishes, candy boxes and pictorial souvenirs.

RMS *Queen Elizabeth* was not completed before World War II and her first service was as a troopship, serving with distinction equal to her sister ship. Similar in size (83,673 tones), speed and appearance, the two liners were easily distinguished by their number of funnels: *Queen Elizabeth* had two; *Queen Mary* three. After the

war the two liners ran weekly shuttles between Great Britain, France and New York. On display at Patriots Point is a 64 inch model, "Plan of First Class Accommodations" dated June 1956, post cards, Cunard playing cards, a candy box and ash tray. Purchased for conversion to a floating university, the ship was destroyed in 1972 by fire while in Hong Kong Harbor and was broken up for scrap.

A competitor of the two Queens just before World War II was the beautiful and fast (29 knots) French liner, *Normandie*. In Atlantic service since 1935, *Normandie* was interned in the United States at the outbreak of war in 1939. The ship was seized 12 December 1942 after Germany declared war on the United States, transferred to the U.S. Navy on the 24th, renamed *Layfayette* and was in the process of conversion to a troopship when she accidentally caught fire in New York harbor 9 February 1942. The 1,029 foot, 54,000 ton liner capsized at the dock, was righted in 1943 but scrapped in 1946 as damage was too extensive and expensive. The Patriots Point exhibit offers a 64 inch model of the liner, a *Layfayette* life preserver and a Normandie bell.

A deck plan, in Italian and English, a brochure, newspaper articles, an art print and dramatic photographs are presently in the museum's collections pertaining to the *Andrea Doria*. On the night of 25 July 1956, the 700 foot, 29,100

Although the NS Savannah is no longer a member of the Patriots Point museum fleet, one of her white life boats was retained. Painted gray, the life boat is now displayed as "Lane Victory Boat 5" to serve as a tangible reminder of the 866 merchant ships, 1,810 Armed Guard and 6,793 seamen lost in World War II. Also, a new Merchant Marine Exhibit on the third deck of Yorktown was completed in 1996.

ton, five year old Italian liner, known as a beautiful ship built around a multitude of priceless paintings and sculptures, was struck by the smaller Swedish-American liner, *Stockholm*, near Nantucket Island. Over 50 died. One of the first disasters to be covered by television, *Stockholm* limped into New York harbor, but *Andrea Doria* slowly rolled to starboard on the 26th and sank into shallow (225 feet) water.

Mine Warfare Display

LOCATED ON *Yorktown's* third deck in a former crews mess is the Mine Warfare Display. An effective offensive and defensive weapon for over 200 years, mines fall into three categories: bottom, moored and drifting. Since 1907, the United States, along with many other countries, has not used drifting mines. Laid by aircraft, submarines and surface vessels, mines have proven especially effective in closing harbors and restricting movement on inland waterways.

The story of the naval mine is told in the Patri-

ots Point display. A significant potion of the story is that no one mine can serve all purposes. Over a dozen examples of various mines are on display, many with cutaway views of the interior. Detonators, batteries, firing mechanisms, relays, coils, terminal boards and other parts of mines are presented in display cases with explanations of their function and operation. The mine warfare display was one of the first exhibits aboard *Yorktown*.

Battle of Charleston Harbor Exhibit

FORT SUMTER, the famous fort operated by the National Park Service, is located on an island. Although admittance to the fort is free, fees are necessary to defray tour boat expenses to reach the island. But, while waiting for the daily two-hour runs aboard one of the boats operated by Fort Sumter Tours, visitors may view the Battle of Charleston Harbor Exhibit located in the breezeway of the Patriots Point Ship's Store and ticket booth.

Fort Sumter was not quite complete on 12

Battle of Charleston Harbor Exhibit

largely intact remains of the *Hunley* were recently discovered not far off Sullivan's Island, and plans are moving forward to raise the historic vessel and place it on display in the Charleston area. Art prints by several artists depict the encounter of the *Hunley* and *Housatonic*, the April 1861 bombardment of Fort Sumter and other scenes that occurred during the four year siege. Storyboards and transparencies educate visitors to the development of the harbor and its role during the Civil War, and a map of the harbor is marked to show major Union and Confederate positions.

April 1961 when Confederate guns began bombardment of the fort in response to President Abraham Lincoln's attempt to replenish supplies within the fort. The Civil War, still remembered as "The War for Southern Independence" by many living south of the Mason-Dixon line, lasted until April 1865. For most of those four years, Fort Sumter was in Confederate hands, being evacuated early in 1865 after General Sherman's army cut supply routes both from Savannah, Georgia, and Columbia, South Carolina. Until the February 1865 abandonment, the fort was constantly bombarded and all but destroyed by Union land and sea forces. The fierce resistance by Confederate defenders was necessary to retain use of the best deep-water port in the South. Many blockade runners made their way into and out of the harbor despite a major Union effort to effectively close the port.

In the Patriots Point exhibit, a documentary video describes the Civil War history of Charleston Harbor. The world's first successful submarine attack occurred in the outer harbor on 17 February 1864 when the Confederate submersible *H.L. Hunley* sank the 207 foot *Housatonic*. The

Also within the exhibit is a seven foot model of the ironclad, CSS *Palmetto State*; three mines used during the Civil War era (Key, Brooks and Singer); an 8 inch Union Parrot incendiary shell, 10 inch Confederate fused shell and an 11 inch Dahlgren solid shot; and six flags. The six flags are the South Carolina state flag, a Confederate naval/battle flag, the first (7 stars) and second (13 stars) national Confederate flags, and 34 star and 35 star Union flags (West Virginia joined the Union in 1863).

Mine Warfare Display.

Over 10,000 people came to Patriots Point to see and board exact replicas of the three vessels that brought Columbus to the new world.

Over 15,000 youth visit Patriots Point each year to participate in the Overnight Camping Program. A favorite experience for the campers is a boat trip to Fort Sumter, site of the beginning of the Civil War.

8

Special Programs

SPECIAL PROGRAMS and events highlight the calendar's of many museums. Although the unique nature of the Patriots Point ship's require a number of permanent exhibits to communicate the history associated with them and their many sister ships, a number of special programs and events have enhanced the museum's educational mission. The process is ongoing and will continue to be, but several special events are presented here to provide perspective.

When mention of "special programs" is made, first remembrance often is that of the annual veteran's reunions, especially those of the *Yorktown*. Usually held over the October Columbus Day holiday weekend, the reunions feature induction's into the Carrier Aviation Hall of Fame and Test Pilot Hall of Honor. Present for these ceremonies or for dedications of new exhibits have been many notables of naval aviation and the surface navy including former President Gerald Ford, several Secretaries of the Navy, a number of CNOs (Chief of Naval Operations), congressmen, and astronauts. De-

stroyer and destroyer escort veterans, however, hold the record for the largest attendance for reunion special events.

From 7 December 1991 through 2 September 1995, numerous programs were presented at Patriots Point in honor and remembrance of the 50th anniversary of significant battles during World War II. The first of these was a Pearl Harbor Remembrance program on 7 December 1991. With over 5,000 attending, tribute was paid to the over 3,000 killed and wounded on that "day of infamy." Present for the ceremony were members of the South Carolina Pearl Harbor Survivors Association and veterans of the Washington (BB-56) Reunion Association. In November 1942 the *Washington* sank the Japanese battleship *Kirishima*, one of the two battle-

Special guests have been a feature of the annual October Yorktown Week. Among those pictured here are former Secretary of the Navy John Lehman, Supreme Court Justice Byron White and the Navy's top World War II ace, Capt. David McCampbell, USN, Ret.

YORKTOWN ASSOCIATION

A group of Pearl Harbor survivors were among the 5,000 present on 7 December 1991 for the 50th anniversary remembrance of the "day of infamy."

Alone with his thoughts in the presence of hundreds, a veteran views the Vietnam Traveling Wall displayed at Patriots Point 8-11 November 1996.

ships that escorted the enemy carriers to Hawaii in December 1941.

The second major World War II remembrance program was held in June 1992, a symposium on the Battle of Midway. Featured were a dozen veterans of the battle, and while public attendance for the program was small, demand for the videotape made during the symposium continues to grow. Several participants have since died and ill health has overtaken others. One can only imagine how popular a videotape would be of U.S. Grant, Robert E. Lee, and Stonewall Jackson. A hundred years from now, students of history will be able to see and hear the late George Gay describe being shot down in his TBD and express his emotions as he witnessed the destruction of Japanese carriers on 4 June 1942. Students will also see and hear "Bert" Earnest describe why he was awarded two Navy Crosses for one flight during the battle, learn how the late fighter pilot Scott McCuskey shot down several Japanese planes, and relive the experience of Dick Best who dropped bombs on two of the enemy carriers.

On 17 April 1993, veterans of the *Yorktown* recreated the commissioning ceremony for their ship. While most of the principals of the 15 April 1943 commissioning were portrayed by others, two repeated their roles for the 50th anniversary ceremony. One, Rear Admiral R.R. Waller, USN, Ret., was *Yorktown's* first executive officer.

On 6 October 1994 fifteen pilots who fought in the 20 October 1944 Battle of the Philippine Sea gathered aboard *Yorktown* for a "Marianas Turkey Shoot" symposium. Representing ten carriers that participated in the battle, several fighter aces, including the fourth leading U.S. Navy ace in World War II, Commander Alex Vraciu, recalled their battle experience as did bomber and torpedo plane pilots.

As interesting as were the programs noted above, none was more emotional than the 8–11 November 1996 visit of "The Wall That Heals," the Vietnam Traveling Wall. Co-sponsored by the Town of Mount Pleasant, The Citadel, Charleston County Schools and a host of other public and private community organizations, all names of the over 58,000 lost in Vietnam were read continuously through the three day observance. Formal observances were made in an opening ceremony, a Charleston County Schools Assembly, a Vietnam Medal of Honor Recipient Tree Planting, and an Interfaith Worship Service.

The all-time attendance record for a special program had nothing to do with aircraft carriers, destroyers, submarines: not even war. In mid–May 1992 three small ships arrived at Patriots Point for a three day stay. Well over 10,000 people flocked to see exact reproductions of the three vessels that brought Christopher Columbus to the new world. While viewing and boarding the decked ship *Santa Maria*, caravels *Pinta* and *Nina*, nearly all visitors commented that they would be hesitant to cross Charleston Harbor in the two smaller vessels and would not attempt to cross the ocean in any of them. Apparent to all was recognition that these exact replicas taught history better than any classroom experience.

The longest running special program is the Overnight Camping Program. In existence nearly

as long as the museum has been open, over 15,000 youth, mostly scout troops, visit Patriots Point annually for periods of one night to a week. Most visits are for a full weekend at which time the campers experience eating and sleeping in the same quarters used by sailors when the *Yorktown* was in commission. Formal presentations are offered along with day trips to Fort Sumter, Fort Moultrie and other Charleston area attractions. The major purpose of this program is to acquaint the present generation of youth to the sacrifice made on their behalf. In time, it will become their responsibility to pass the story of naval history and sacrifice to a subsequent generation.

A Japanese plane falls during the June 1942 Battle of the Philippine Sea, often recalled as the "Marianas Turkey Shoot." USN

Veteran pilots who fought in the Battle of the Philippine Sea offered remembrances during a June 1992 symposium. Yorktown (CV-10) *participated in the overwhelming victory.*

Charleston County school students join Vietnam veterans
and Medal of Honor recipients to plant trees on the Patriots Point grounds.

One of the special programs at Patriots Point was a visit from renowned
entertainer Bob Hope. Mixed with his humor during this 1990 visit were his
recollections of being aboard Yorktown *when the carrier was in active service.*

9

Benefactors

OVER THE YEARS, Patriots Point has received substantial gifts of money and service from individuals and reunion associations. To demonstrate appreciation, Patriots Point created the Benefactor Memorial Program in September 1990. Into 1997, the following individuals have been recognized for their generosity: Vice Admiral Vincent de Poix, USN, Ret., (first commanding officer of the first nuclear aircraft carrier, *Enterprise* CVAN-65); Captain James B. Cain, USN, Ret., (WWII ace and commanding officer of *Yorktown* CV-10, 1965-66); Captain John Thyr Sorensen, USN, Ret., (Dental Officer aboard *Yorktown* during World War II); Captain William Alden Hall, USN, Ret., (Commanding Officer of *Oklahoma* BB-37, 1935-37); H.A. "Hank" Pyzdrowski, (Avenger pilot on *Gambier Bay* CVE-73); John Payne (veteran of *Essex* CV-9); Philip Gilbert (veteran of *Princeton* CVL-23); Chester Bacon (15 battle stars on his Asiatic Pacific campaign medal); Harold Walter Syfrett (Yorktown Association chaplain); Col. Dennis Dewitt Nicholson, Jr. and Martin L. Tauber (veteran of *Yorktown* CV-10).

THE FOLLOWING ORGANIZATIONS are recognized for their generosity: *Hancock* CV, CVA-19 (two plaques, one honoring all who served aboard during World War II, and a second in memory of all association deceased members); *Langley* CVL-27 (nine battle stars in WWII); *Ticonderoga* CV/CVA-14 (three Navy Unit Commendations for Vietnam service); *Hobson* DD-464, DMS-26 (Presidential Unit Citation for WWII); *John C. Butler* DE-339 (Presidential Unit Citation for WWII); and Fighting Squadron 13 (VF-13) of World War II fame.

Past and Current Members of the Patriots Point Development Authority Board of Directors, 1973–1999

L. Wayne Adams
George E. Campsen, Jr.
A. Crawford Clarkson, Jr.
Jesse A. Coles, Jr.
Alex C. Crouch
R. Gordon Darby
Charles E. Eiserhardt, Jr.
John F. Floyd
Joseph P. Griffith

J.E. Guerry, Jr.
J. Mat Hiers
Tee Hooper, Jr.
Charles F. Hyatt
Harold Jacobs
Leroy H. Keyserling
James T. Lazar
Theodore T. Mappus, Jr.
J. A. Meetze

Charles T. Mauro
H.E. Pearce, Jr.
E.B. Purcell
Charles T. Oakley
Myrtle C. Riggs
Horace L. Tilghman, Jr.
Debra A. Turner
James Elliott Williams
Cheryll N. Woods-Flowers

*Seated from left: Rear Admiral James H. Flatley III, CEO, and Tee Hooper, Jr.,
Chairman, Patriots Point Board of Directors.
Standing from left: Debra Turner; William E. Craver III (Legal Counsel); Wayne Adams;
Harold Jacobs, Vice Chairman; Mayor Cheryll N. Woods-Flowers.
Absent from photograph, J. A. Meetze.*